BROKEN PIECES

RACHEL THOMPSON

Booktrope Editions
Seattle, WA 2013

Cover Design by Loretta Matson

Edited by Jessica Swift Eldridge

PRINT ISBN 978-1-62015-160-0

EPUB ISBN 978-1-62015-256-0

Library of Congress Control Number: 2013922179

TABLE OF CONTENTS

ABOUT THE AUTHOR

Rachel Thompson (aka **RachelintheOC**) is a bestselling author and social media/author marketing consultant.

Her three books, A Walk In The Snark, The Mancode: Exposed and Broken Pieces are all #1 Kindle bestsellers! Midwest Book Review and two Amazon Top 10 Hall of Fame reviewers all gave Broken Pieces five stars!

When not writing, she helps authors and other professionals with branding and social media for her company, BadRedhead Media. Her articles appear regularly in the San Francisco Book Review (BadRedhead Says...), 12Most.com, bitrebels.com, Self-Publishers Monthly, and BookPromotion.com.

Rachel hates walks in the rain, running out of coffee, and coconut. She lives in California with her family.

FOREWORD

In 1972, comedian Jerry Lewis took a huge departure from his traditional comedic roles when he directed and starred in *The Day the Clown Died*. This film was anything but funny and, unfortunately, was never finished because funding for it was cut after only a month into production. Perhaps people didn't want to see Lewis in any other light than they had seen him thus far. Rather than accept him as a man and actor with diverse interests and tastes, it's likely he was pigeonholed into the only thing he'd been known as — funny.

I mention this because Rachel Thompson's new book is a total departure from her two previous humor books, *A Walk in the Snark* and *The Mancode: Exposed*. Sure, I did laugh at *The Mancode*. Now I want this *on the record* that my female friends and family who read Rachel's books with her wry observations commented, "Yeah, Bennet, she got you nailed and down pat!"

Known for her humor, satire, and wit, Thompson has embarked on a different journey with this book. While this book deviates from the styles she's been known for thus far, it is still *her*.

We all have dark sides. As much as we all love to laugh and feel good, there are things in our pasts that haunt us. Or worse yet, things that we refuse to or simply cannot look at. Rachel, however, does just this. She looks at her experiences with bravery, honesty, and a raw truth. This dramatic collection is an emotional flaying that you will not just read, you will feel. The pages of this book have pieces of Rachel's soul imprinted on them.

Feelings can get twisted when you open yourself to old wounds you thought you may have closed. It's hard to bring raw emotions to a printed page. I know, I did it myself when I wrote my memoir. *Broken Pieces* shows one woman's journey through life, the bad, the ugly, and the worst of it. But she shows us light, too. To truly know dark, you must know light. Rachel's book is a testament to this.

I hope you enjoy this book and take away the passion and love that Rachel has put on these pages.

— Bennet Pomerantz
Columnist <u>AUDIOWORLD</u>
Columnist <u>To Be or What</u>
Columnist A Piece of My Mind (Night Owl Reviews)
Host <u>ANYTHING GOES</u> Blog Talk radio

INTRODUCTION

Write something you'd never show your mother or father.

— Author Lorrie Moore

This is a book about fracture. About the experiences that make up a life. About the pieces of me.

Delving into naked emotion is a terrifying proposition. Digging into our souls to look for answers that may not be there is a ledge most of us avoid.

And yet, here I am.

This book is set up so you can read it all the way through, or an essay at a time. Read a few, walk away. I've set the book up how I experienced it, how these pieces came to me, in an organic order that makes sense to me.

My hope is to touch a nerve, make you think, make you *feel*.

My journey will take you to familiar places many often shy away from. It might be hard to read. Some of the pieces were hard to write. What I experienced stayed inside me, waiting for me to learn how to tell it on the other side of time.

And now it's here for you — in the raw.

CAGED

The right answer is to turn and walk away. But his arms are so strong and his words caress her soul. In his heat she abandons her resolve.

She's unsure how it started, moving from found to lost. One day she watches birds fly on apathetic wings, the next he stands behind her — his hands inside her heart.

He damages her new home, where she now lays her head, the place where guilt and lust meet.

But she cannot leave. His eyes hold her captive.

"You are mine," he tells her. "I own you now." She doesn't disagree.

Her breath quickens, her skin burns from the real and imagined hold he has on her. He whispers promises of life together, as long as all the pieces of her are his.

Pieces of her —

all he needs.

CHINA DOLL

I felt the storm break my heart.

Maybe I knew he had taken his life before I got the call; perhaps even before he left, his words a warning I didn't know to catch.

I can admit that now.

Before he died, when we spoke a storm brewed in his words. He had lost so many people—some he hated, some he loved. But still. So many deaths. Drinking ruined him; alcohol killed his marriage, twisted his relationship with his young son into sadness. He only told me bits and pieces. His language, sparse, as if he had created his own. I gleaned as much as I could from every conversation, trying to understand unspoken words, held breaths.

If only I had read between his lines.

If I closed my eyes, could I have touched his words?

"SEE WHO I AM NOW!" He angrily shouted, though his rage was couched between desire and love.

"I'm not that man anymore who would hurt you. You're my china doll, baby."

He carried me for twenty years, freezing me in time; taking me out, looking at me, before putting me back on his shelf. Who he thought I was. Not realizing I would grow and change, becoming a different person. A stronger person. A doll who didn't break quite so easily.

The mind warps what time can't forget. But I will never forget.

And I am not his doll. I am not fragile.

Then again, I'm not the one who broke.

LIGHT

Allow me to drape my limbs over you; my secret murmurs soothing fears that keep you awake as the rays of the day fade on borrowed rest.

Grasping your hand to keep you from losing your way back to me, you meet my eyes with a rush of desire that slams me in a hard, brilliant flash.

Do you hear me? I whisper along your skin, cooled by the night air. Crossing this wide river to you, I pray you'll reach for me as I pass by, drowning in your depths.

You, my only salvation.

Will you save me?

Waiting for the sun, I barely breathe so as not to wake you, unable to turn away from the glare of what we've wrought.

I bathe in our entangled gleam, where love lives inside the knowledge that tomorrow fades again.

Illumination only lasts until darkness decides to fall.

BIRD

He found me, waiting and bruised, pushing his way so deeply inside me; I never thought he'd find his way out.

But he surprised us both, shoving me aside as quickly as he'd come. Using, abusing, he feared his inner darkness would disrupt our carefully structured nest.

Scared our pleasure would eat at his soul.

Too afraid to give room, or care, or thought, he left me as he found me, waiting and bruised, but now also willing and broken.

I shakily tend my wounds, mystified if I had flown, or fallen.

AND THEN I LET HIM GO

It hits me at the strangest times.

The fact that someone who was a part of my life is gone. *Here today, gone tomorrow.* A concept so hard to grasp when it happens to —

To whom? He's the one who took his own life. Nothing happened to me, his ex-love from many years ago.

We spoke earlier that day. The day he decided would be his last.

We never will again. Impossible.

But he visits me, in my dreams, conjured by my disbelieving subconscious.

Or is he conjured by my heart?

I wake up from the dreams confused and — somehow — relieved. In some, he tells me he's OK. In others he doesn't speak, but he shows me he's fine.

But there's still too much I don't know or understand about the man he became — this man I once shared my heart and body with. So I go about my days now, my full life bursting with my own family, and when he visits me in my dreams, I let him in.

And then I let him go.

ROOMS

Women have rooms inside of us men cannot fathom.

It's where we store the depths of the hurt we've been dealt.

Where we store the deep love we never want to lose.

Where we've tucked away all those cutting comments through the years, when we couldn't react because we had company. The place where we shoved the painful words down, swallowed the reactions and put them in the corner; pushing it all back down when it threatened to rise up,; afraid the tentative piece of string might snap and all the hurtful words he sent your way will tumble back out and hit him so hard he won't comprehend the language you're speaking is his own.

We fold our stories inside ourselves.

We unwrap them when nobody is looking.

We carry former lovers, long lost, inside our limbs. We feel their caresses, remember exactly how their tongues entwined with ours as our bodies melted, their eyes on ours as they entered us; even our cells remember the exquisite burn.

A woman never forgets, though she may learn to love another. We wrap those memories away for safekeeping, even when those lovers hurt and brutalize, our hearts break and we cry forever tears. We have a room for that pain, a special key we hide to lock it away.

Women grow, our hearts accommodating all the players in our lives.

We explore our rooms often, sometimes inadvertently. Our hearts won't allow us to ignore our secret places for long. Try as we might to suppress our desires, our unknown thoughts and fears will rise to guide us to different places, new rooms we never knew existed but were within us the whole time.

Embrace. Hold tight while you dance. Jump.

Our rooms are buried so deeply, many times we don't listen or can't hear. We fall, search, drift, let go. We hold our breath, worry what others will think, lose ourselves.

Don't.

Women have rooms inside us.

Breathe.

FEAR DOES NOT OWN ME

This essay is about fear. How it shapes us. The impressions it makes on our souls.

Some events are so harrowing, they either shape who we become or we move past them. They either break us entirely, or we pick up the pieces and put ourselves back together, altered but not shattered.

Our neighbor molested me when I was a child, just twelve years old. The same age my daughter is now.

A dad, he had girls of his own. Not just once, and not only me.

What happened *happened.* I focused on my studies, athletics, family and friends. I did not let this experience hold me back in any way, though it always lurked inside me—in my body and in my mind. I didn't share it with people, of course.

Who wants to talk about something like that?

When I had a daughter of my own, the real anxiety set in. I didn't even realize what was happening, to be honest. Though I returned to work, the thought of trusting my precious baby to a total stranger made my world turn gray, colored only by fear.

Taking that leap of faith, trusting someone to not harm my child the way I had been hurt, completely took over my thought process, even when I wasn't aware of it. Consumed by terrible thoughts and fear of the unknown, I stopped functioning. At all.

I got help. It's easier for women to admit we cannot do everything, particularly at a time when so much is going on.

I refused to be shattered, irreparably shattered, by something that happened TO me, that I had no control over.

I somehow realized once I wandered into the darkest recesses of my soul — the place I never wanted to be, the place I thought I safely locked and kept in an untouchable part of me — that to be the best mom I could be, I first had to be my best self.

And I write. I always, always write.

I own my fear, but my fear does not own me.

FIGHT OR FLIGHT

After he killed himself, I pulled out my old journals. From two of our over-four-plus-years together.

Once you do that, there's no turning back.

I wonder if telling my future self the emotional rollercoaster would have made a difference, would have been worth it? As I read each page, I couldn't help but think, *that poor girl*. Why put up with All. That. Crap?

Sweet, loving, he even talked of our future at times. Perhaps it's what kept me coming back all those years. Bites of the apple. This game of push and pull kept me hungry.

But I ignored many signs. He drank. A lot. Back then we called it "partying," cause that's what we did. Early twenties is the time to do that, right? When he drank, he opened up to me emotionally and what chick doesn't thrive on that?

Then he got one DUI. Then another. My future self would tell my young self what came to be true: that alcohol would ruin him.

Many people say forget the past. It's the past for a reason. And to be honest, I forgot A LOT of it. I packed those journals away in a box that I hadn't seen for twenty years. After I broke it off with him, I hadn't seen or heard from D at all. Moving three thousand miles away helped a lot, of course. As did marrying my guy.

All this would probably have stayed in the recesses of my mind if he hadn't contacted me on Facebook out of the blue one day. A simple message, "What's up, Rach?" turning me to jelly.

Surprised by my visceral reaction, my body immediately remembered *our pattern*.

Checking messages while walking in to pick up my kids from school, my legs began to shake so badly I had to sit down. A friend came over to see what happened. Clearly, whatever memories I had tucked away were tumbling around inside, fighting for position in my mind; I couldn't focus on any particular one.

My body became a swirling mass of nerves. Fight or flight, sympathetic nervous system action, the chemical feedback starting on its own.

How could this be a good thing?

Calling my husband, I told him about the message. Of course he knew my history with this guy. A big believer in closure, my reaction made sense to him. Sure, I broke it off with D but I never understood why a protective man, so supposedly obsessively in love with me, would cheat. It just never added up—so many unanswered questions I set aside, buried, not wanting to waste any more time down a useless road that led to only pain.

My husband suggested I do whatever I thought right, and understood if I wanted to reconnect.

Not entirely sure, I knew my charged reaction meant I couldn't just stuff this dizzying collection of emotions back into a box. So D and I began to speak online. No sunflower, I wanted to know: why did you cheat? Humble, apologetic ... and single.

Barking up the wrong tree, pal.

It fascinated me how easily we fell back into our pattern ... How quickly he'd try to control my actions and behaviors, even though we were no longer in a relationship. I didn't have to put up with it anymore and I'd give him a hard time. I don't think only his ego brought him back to me, though. As I would find out a mere three months later, not all in his life was...

As it seemed.

LINES

It's never a good idea to date someone you work with. Everybody knows that. Still, lots of people do it.

D and I were no exception. The temptation too great. We were young (nineteen), single, why not? We enjoyed working together — a way to spend more time flirting and being silly.

He entered the management program, so we shook on the deal: no hanky panky at work. Seemed easy enough. Especially because we worked on different days. Late one night in bed, D told me: "Keep work at work and play at play, babe." I thought I understood, except: what about work parties? Or just hanging out with work friends in our off time? A drugstore like ours maintained a very social atmosphere and people hung out together a lot after work.

Where do we draw the line?

Across my heart. He became so good at holding my body close and then pushing me away as though he was punishing me for loving him. I didn't know when to gasp for air. And thus began my unknowing addiction.

I took whatever hits he gave me: snippets of time, love, kisses, notes, rare phone calls, even fights, and eventually, the slow, inevitable rip of my soul when he cheated on me with a coworker's friend at a party I couldn't attend because I had to work. I found out from a shy male coworker named Joe, who thought I should know.

Cheating. One little word that carries so much meaning. One little word that takes away your trust, your self-esteem. It erases what you think your life is.

No matter how hard I tried to ignore it, there was no escaping the fact that he chose another girl while with me. This truth created a stone in my stomach, one I couldn't purge. I was physically changed — forever. Everywhere I went, this stony weight accompanied me. I couldn't get away.

Walk away, or stay? While he stepped on the broken pieces of my soul, I walked forward to my inevitable decision.

Confronting him, he acted extraordinarily loving and sweet, something I recognized as his typical behavior of regret. He hung his head while the excuse "I was drunk" dripped so easily from his lips. Scars started forming their jagged lines inside my veins, a protection from future assaults.

Sure, alcohol makes you do stupid things, but there's one thing even I knew in that moment: your heart doesn't allow you to separate people into neat categories of convenience like 'work' and 'play.' A good heart takes responsibility for what your brain cannot.

Accepting the sting of these new raw scars, I walked out his door, seeing in his eyes as I looked back that I wasn't the only one with a new addiction.

Knowing those lines had merged.

MISTAKES

College, 1983

I'm a sophomore, nineteen years old.

Bill, a nice enough guy from one of my journalism classes, invites me to a party at this frat, I say yes. (*Mistake #1*: his turf).

I go with a girlfriend in her car. (*Mistake #2*: always drive your own car). I didn't know him very well and, not into the whole Greek scene anyway, I didn't get super dressed up: jeans and a cute top. Flats, since he was on the short side. Mostly, I was happy to be out of my room and not studying for once.

My girlfriend's a sorority sister, so she floats into the room on her pink fluff of air-kisses and vapor. With my writer's eye, I observe the mating rituals going on around me while I figure out how many beers it's gonna take me to either fit in with this Ralph Lauren crowd or scope out who's got the weed.

I decide two beers is a good number. Bill shows up. I know this by the he-man grip he places on my arm. (*Mistake #3*: underestimating a dude's strength based on size). Though not a big guy, he is lean and wiry. He wrestles for the school and repeatedly asked me to watch his matches.

Bill is charming and a smooth talker. We chat for an hour or two. He reaches to hold my hand. Friendly, sweet. I need to use the bathroom so he escorts me through the crowd. "Hey, use this one back here. No one knows about it. I used to live here so I know this house backward and forward," he tells me. Because I *really, really* have to pee, I let him lead me by the hand into a room where I thought the other bathroom was.

MISTAKE NUMBER FOUR — trusting that he is the nice guy he appears to be. Why should I think anything different? Why wouldn't I trust a nice, helpful guy, who had gone out of his way to be sweet?

He locks the door so fast I hardly see him do it. I quickly realize that something isn't right, then he throws me on the bed and pins me with one knee. His face is unrecognizable, like a monster's, teeth bared, inhuman.

* * *

I didn't wear sexy clothes that night. I didn't do anything other than spend time with a guy who played the part of a decent guy from one of my classes. We hadn't even kissed.

Yet there he was, tearing at my clothes, hitting me, unzipping his pants. My heart beat so loudly, I could hear it in my mouth.

It didn't happen, though. There's a "happy" ending. Why? Because I fought. I kicked, I bit, I scratched, I screamed. Did I *think* it would make a difference? I don't know, because I didn't think. Not until later.

Not until after.

They say once your heart rate goes above two hundred beats a minute, your problem-solving abilities go out the window. You're acting purely on instinct. Adrenaline kicks in.

I guess it was a combination of factors that ended his attempt: my reaction, people hearing my screams and knocking on the door, and the fact that I drew blood when I scratched his face. It seemed that making him bleed sobered him up, made him human again.

He told me he would deny everything, of course. And yes, he told me I'd been "asking for it."

Facing him in class that Monday—he with a bandage on his cheek, me covered in bruises—is still one of the toughest things I've ever done.

Back in the early-80s, the term "date-rape" didn't exist—or at least not in a well-known or accepted manner. In fact, the term 'date rape' was first used in a September 1982 article in Ms. Magazine.

Sadly, I didn't know what had happened to me. Conventional wisdom at that time: I had nothing to report but fighting off some jerk. My visible proof?

A ripped top, some nasty bruises. It's the proof you can't see that creates invisible scarring.

However, I take pride in the fact that I fought back against an enemy that, at that time, had no name.

RELEASE

I gave my heart to a man who loved me, who wanted to be with me. Who ultimately was afraid of all I offered.

I didn't understand why he sabotaged our future at the time — cheating on me, again, as we were making final plans to move in together. By the time he came over to smooth talk his way out of it, I was *done*. No more crying. Even my tears had given up on him. I'd already moved on, his cheating was simply the key left in the mailbox.

Many times I've looked back on that time as a metamorphosis. He kept me in a cocoon, really. His jealousy so intense, he often checked my messages to see if other guys had called. He once threw wineglasses at his apartment wall in a fit of rage when I told him I was going to a concert with a platonic male study partner.

Whining with remorse, apologizing as he picked glass out of my hair, I knew then that whatever secrets he whispered in my ear, I no longer wanted to keep.

Of course, I allowed it to happen, completely losing myself in him. A willing partner, I knew his sweet side. I was special, the only one privy to the protective silk nobody else could see. And I was in love with that? An elusive wisp I almost never got to see. Yet that glimpse was enough for me to continue to search for warmth inside his arms.

In our tiny microcosm, where time melted as I fell deeper in, where I became the girlfriend he wanted me to be, I should have known better. I knew that meeting a platonic friend would upset him, but I did it anyway. A small act of rebellion on my part, which earned me shards of glass on my head. But I also got back a piece of myself — my strength — through my defiance.

It took me awhile, but I finally saw the only future we could have — a tapestry of glass woven with lies and tears.

RULES

Things are not always how they seem. Will you be ready?

     — "2-1", Imogen Heap

I spoke with him at lunch. By dinner, he had pointed a gun to his chest and pulled the trigger.

Suicide is devastating for those left behind. I'm not his family. No longer lovers though still connected by invisible wires and time.

Did I have the right to grieve?

Grief has no rules, though people attach order to it. *Wear this. Go here. Say this. Don't say that.*

Many people, to this day, tell me how I *should* feel. Everyone has an opinion about *my* emotions. Mostly it goes, "Thank God you were no longer with him. Aren't you glad you dumped him! Better him than you. You should be thankful such garbage is out of your life. I hope you're not sad. He was a loser. Don't let him bring you down." Like that.

I don't think people mean to intentionally scratch the heart I try so hard not to wear on my sleeve.

In a surreal gift from the universe, time both stands still and flies past you in that singular moment when you find out someone you once loved is gone.

I never once regretted my decision to leave him. He hurt me; his flaws proved too great. Not only him, not only me: *we* were flawed. A man I once loved with all my being ended his life in a violent, tragic way. That leaves an imprint on your soul. But it also taught me how to restructure the fractured pieces of my grief into an understanding of my own grieving rules—ones that are not dictated by anyone else. They are my rules that work for me.

And now I've made my own rules:

It's okay to be sad that he suffered so greatly he felt he had no other option. It's okay to ignore what other people believe I should or shouldn't say or feel about my ex-love's suicide. Most of them aren't in my shoes.

It's okay to write about it. I don't need anyone's permission to write.

While I understand his death isn't about me, it's okay to feel and explore the impact his life has had on me, particularly the recent reconnection we shared. Many are upset by this. That's okay, too.

People have their own unique ways of dealing with their grief. I've learned, however, that no one owns my grief but me.

Suicide is a reality. It's up to those of us left behind to examine the pieces and then keep on living our lives — our own way.

Sanctuary

Her need for him so razor sharp it hits her gut and she doubles over, the pain of longing moving so piercingly through her she's not sure she'll ever get past her craving or intense yearning.

One night. Their bodies at turns melted so sweetly, tenderly. Other times there were fires so hot they were slick with the sweat of an effortless heat that blistered with their touch.

Three a.m., their violet hour, waking to find their bodies fit with no words, only the perfect spoon of her into him. No need for any more questions of whether they were meant to be. Her skin absorbed him as if she always knew he'd been waiting for her. He breathed her in, branding the scent of her deep inside his heart.

He moves above her, their eyes on each other as he enters her soul.

How they came to be, neither of them is sure. They only know something more powerful than they could ever hope to understand brought them together.

But theirs was an understanding beyond words.

And here they are.

Living the surface of each day, skating on a few stolen words. Desire grows to a fevered pitch, buzzing even when they subconsciously share thoughts across the miles.

Owning each other wholly. Her eyes, his light.

His arms, her sanctuary.

SHADOWS

I won't forget the night
He held me to his side.
Too many tokes. Too many shots.
Too many hours lost in each other's skin.
Couldn't sleep.
Couldn't eat.
We simply touched.
Looking past the dingy grey apartment walls,
Holding no memories, no warmth.
Peering into the ocean of his eyes,
Wondering at the pain he held there.
Asking for his soul to let me in.
A kiss his reply —
Vanquishing my thoughts.
His fingers, dancing in millimeters,
Full of heat.

A party at his place.
Men like moths
Pressing around me.
The only reason I can think of
That made him want me so close,
It hurt to breathe.
Showing his strength, his power …
His boldness sweet candy,
To a lost little girl
Hungry for more.

Morning came, I rose to dress.
He grabbed my arm.
"Don't go."
The look of pleading
Like waves in his eyes.
I knew then —
There would be more sleepless nights.
Darkness spreading its taint,
Whispering its secret:
We were beyond too late.
He was lying in the bed he'd made.

Not sure what he clung to
That last night.
I saw it later,
I see it now.
I close my eyes, feeling the sharp edges on his skin,
Knowing
He traded my love for
Another green-eyed girl's.
Feeling his shards poking through
The shadows of my heart.

TOUCH

She feels his hands holding her soul.
Keeping the garden of her emotions,
Close inside his fist.
Meeting her rush of words
With a silent finger.
Shhhh.

Guarding his heart,
Brushing aside all that matters,
With his clear-eyed gaze.
He grasps her fire,
Before watching
It slowly fall.

Dusting off her tears,
Work to be done.
He knows but can't see,
What he can't hold.
She turns, waiting,
Urgent for his touch.

He clasps in his hands
What he can't deny,
And doesn't question.
It's what he doesn't
Carry anymore,
That cages him.

They walk along the shore,
Folding her heart in his hands.
He keeps it with him,
In the pages of his journal,
A bookmark keeping his place
Hidden, mislaid.

She used to be so strong,
Never handing over her love.
But he's taken her, filled her;
His slave, his mercy.
Her heart so raw; he doesn't know
She's already lost.

Two Minutes

There are crystalline moments that stand out in our memories: happy, sad, evocative, and those bright, adrenaline-filled flashes that come out of nowhere yet singe themselves in the lining of our subconscious. Invaders of the contented.

Getting pregnant, carrying a child. The entire process is wrought with unknowns for first-time parents. Some have it easier than others, as was the case with my first — easy. I had a bit of trouble conceiving, though we didn't have to resort to fertility drugs. It was really just a matter of my age (35) and timing (work schedules). When it happened, we were thrilled.

Already married seven years, my husband and I decided we were finally settled, well-traveled, ready for a child. My pregnancy was fairly normal and easy, as was my labor. After four hours of pushing, my daughter Anya was pulled from me. The whole room got suddenly, eerily quiet.

"Why isn't she crying?" I nervously asked my doctor. Where were my husband, my mom, and the entire group of people who just seconds ago were so ebulliently surrounding my nether regions? My dad, standing near my head, reassuringly patting my cheek. "I don't know, dolly," he said soothingly. And we waited. And waited, and waited, for someone, *anyone*, to speak.

"Someone please tell me what's going on with my baby!" I heard myself scream in a howling, primal growl. Fear gripped my body so completely that my legs started to cramp and I could no longer speak.

The pain of birth forgotten. Fear became my pain. Anya had a "slow transition," which basically means she was slow to take her own first spontaneous breaths and needed help. She was soon fine but those first two minutes of her life were terrifying. The longest two minutes of my life. I will never forget a room full of people working so silently over a tiny, seven-pound new life taken from my body.

My husband said he couldn't look at or even talk to me during those two minutes because he knew the bond between mother and daughter was already so strong—after all, I had carried this precious life to fruition. His fear for what would happen to me, if something happened to her, was too overwhelming. He was at a loss. He went to the baby instead and did everything he could to help those amazing doctors and nurses who flooded our room within seconds of the call.

I'll be forever grateful. I still get chills thinking about that day almost thirteen years ago.

Fear protects us. It's a valuable emotion in some ways, because it bonds you to those you love.

Fear does not let you ever forget.

SPINNING

"I'm pretty sure they call it *Spin The Bottle* for more than the obvious reasons."

At least, that's what I told my older sister after I received my very first French kiss.

"Okay, back up. Um, what?" She looked at me in confusion. "I get the kissing part. I mean, der. But why another reason?" She asked me with trepidation both in her voice and on her freckled fifteen-year old face.

See, I was about twelve years old at this point — two years into my burgeoning career as a writer. I not only questioned each situation, I also wrote down every last detail, which unfortunately included recording my sister's recent bout of "illness" after an evening out with her girlfriends, which ended with her throwing up in the aluminum milk can (oh so popular in the seventies) that stood next to her bed.

She still hadn't forgiven me for leaving my incriminating notebook evidence open on my desk (hey, milk and cookies called). Arguing that the horrific smell was evidence enough (despite her teen logic, apparently just putting the lid on a milk can does not mask the smell of alcohol-laced vomit) was still not flying with her.

In all honesty, I couldn't really blame her for wondering why I was questioning the validity of the classic *Spin The Bottle* tradition, given its tried and true trustworthiness. Yet here I was.

Rebel.

Not sure I could adequately explain, given the surreal nature of my experience, I tried as best I could to tell her about my sleepover at Sunday School Jew Camp the night before.

*   *   *

Somehow the counselors (teenagers themselves) had left us campers alone long enough for us to indulge in a quick and dirty game of Bottle —

four guys, four girls, in the dark with a flashlight, in the synagogue lobby. (If Jews believed in hell we would probably burn in it, but hey, with the exception of some cool Old Testament thoughts on the afterlife, we figured we were golden.)

It was on.

I ended up, after losing a dare, shoved into the arms of a decent-looking, dark-haired bar-mitzvahed boy (well, I suppose I should say man?) named Edmund. Our instruction from bossy Deirdre Greenburg was simple: don't come back until you've tongued.

Hand in hand, we walked down the hall. He was kinda cute, I had to admit.

As we shuffled to our doom, hearts beating louder than footsteps, intrepid but still the littlest bit shy, I asked him, "Have you ever done this before?"

He stopped, leaned against the wall, and with one arm around my waist, gently pulled me toward him. He put his hand on my cheek in a soft caress, drawing my mouth toward his. I tried to quiet the thoughts that raced through my mind as our tongues met and began to touch, exploring.

It was electric. A jolt coursing through my body, a heat I had never experienced before. The sensation so intense, the cliché of the earth moving under my feet made sense. I understood the song now. My head began to spin. It was a good thing he was holding on to me, as I think I began to fall a little.

He pulled back, a satisfied smile on his face as he answered, "I have now."

My sister stared at me, open-mouthed.

"Lucky duck. My first kiss made me want to throw up in my milk can."

FLUTTERS

She feels dead inside. He was there when she fell asleep.

Gone when she awoke.

That's what she'll always remember. Not that he's gone. Because that will never change. That she can accept.

No, what she can't accept is that she was there. He was with her, by her side, entwined in her limbs, hand in hand. And still she didn't know.

His heart, her heart.

Still she couldn't stop him.

She had breathed him all night. His scent of wood, wax, strength, sweetness, love, possession, desire, and sex — she buried herself in his neck as she always did, her favorite place in the world. She claimed her spot, not that he ever minded. His fingers would play up and down her back, massaging her in circles, relaxing her into sleep.

Her inhale, his exhale.

She woke up to find him gone; her favorite drink, his special blend of green tea and lavender, next to her on the bedside table. He knew she loved the scent. He knew she liked to start her day slowly, quietly.

As she took her first sip, she noticed the flutter of papers floating by. Had he left the window open? He was always so careful to lock up. Her body chilled. The first sign something wasn't right, so incredibly not right. Her subconscious knew then what the warning scrap of paper was trying to say.

He's not coming back. She grabbed a scrap; symbols, drops of red. It made no sense. Her heart sank. She knew it didn't matter. The lavender scent took on a rank metallic stench, making her want to retch.

She dropped the cup, watching the tea stain their much-derided white carpet.

She wondered — *If I had woken up, would I have smelled his sadness, his desperation, and his detachment?*

His death, her breath.

He told her once, she remembers, these two words have no other rhyme but each other.

If she could go back, she thinks —

She would open her eyes, instead of her heart.

THE PIED PIPER

On the sheriffs' second visit to our home, they brought a female officer with them. "She's better with little girls," someone told my mom.

The police wanted to know the truth. They told us "Don't be ashamed. You didn't do anything wrong." It was the big man. He was the one in trouble.

I was twelve years old. My older sister was thirteen. My baby sister was just that, only one. I held her close, all dark curly hair and soft velvety skin.

"Has he touched you inappropriately?" I whispered to my mom, "What does that word mean?" All she could do was cry and squeeze my shoulder. It hurt when she did that.

My mom said, "We called him the 'Pied Piper' for God's sake." The sheriffs looked down at their shiny black shoes.

The female sheriff asked if they could talk with each girl separately. My parents were terrified.

So was I. A twelve-year-old girl with a terrible burden. I'd protected my family for the past three months and they didn't even know. I'd kept them alive and they had no idea.

That...that man. My best friend's daddy. Yes. He took me on scooter rides to the isolated trees down the street. Yes, he'd done things. Yes, more than once. He showed me his gun, with the bullets. Made me hold it.

He told me he'd kill my family if I told on him. Told me sometimes fear is the best friend we could ever have. I start to cry. "I don't want my family to die."

The lady sheriff's eyes burn a hole in my soul. She knows. She knows what he did to me.

My mom is confused, then she realizes; I already knew what inappropriate meant.

LOST

I know it's time to sleep. I know it's time to dream.

When you left me I crawled into bed and craved sleep so I could dream of you.

You came to me then, holding me with your strong, muscular arms so tightly I was afraid to breathe for fear I'd wake up.

Because if I woke up, you'd be gone.

Again.

In my dreams, you're here. With me. Breathing me in.

Holding my words in your eyes, entwined like the strings of my shattered heart.

Your fingers burn my fears away, pressing tracks on my skin to show me you'll never leave again.

How much would I give to carry those scars with me now?

I cry when I wake, aching for one reminder — just one — to help me through these endless, yawning days without you.

Night my only refuge, my only way to find you inside my soul.

OF BATS AND MEN

You just do not know what people in groups are capable of until you witness violence first hand.

A group of my friends and I jumped in my car to go hang out one night with all the school kids in an area called "The Courts," which was simply a name for a group of streets (ergo, courts) under development in the suburbs of Sacramento. This was probably circa 1980.

Piled into my trusty Datsun 1200 that my dad had splurged all of $800 on, we tooled on over, found our posse and toked up one little joint. Within minutes, we heard yelling and saw some guys from school running toward us, wild-eyed and clearly afraid. Behind them were adult men with baseball bats, running and cursing.

Because our reality was a bit warped anyway, it took us a second to realize that Baseball Bat Men were not just after the guys, but all of us. We made it into my car with the sound of glass smashing around us, as the bat-wielding maniacs laid waste a few cars behind us.

My not-rod decided to pick that moment to not freakin' start (thanks, Dad), so I sustained a hit to the bumper from one of the bat-bearers (protecting their turf from little girl sophomores is apparently hard work). Eventually the engine putt-putted to life and we were off, at 10 mph — high speeds to get away with our lives.

Tears and screams accompanied my driving as we decided what the hell to do. Returning home to my house and telling my fairly cool parents was the chosen path. Unfortunately, the 'rents were in the middle of a dinner party. But they didn't care — they called the sheriff, dad took us back over, and the police closely surveyed the area, acting the part of weary law-enforcement officers who had seen it all. Yep, something had indeed taken place based on evidence in the street. Of course, the maniacal bat-wielders were long gone. The sheriff and my dad said they were probably upset neighbors tired of the noise.

We learned that even though The Courts were open streets, *we were* technically trespassing *and* loitering. We were the criminals? Yep. Aw, hell. (Most kids don't tell their parents but I figured there was no way around the bumper, so I might as well 'fess up.)

It was terrifying, but in the end, we were all just fine. Scared and a bit smarter, perhaps.

REBOUND GUY

It's not a conscious thing. We don't sit in front of our mirror and say, *yeah, I need a rebound guy* as we put our makeup on.

The rebound guy will put back the pieces of our shattered heart. Pieces crushed into fine glass powder, scraped carefully into our shiny compact, our new lover's lips bleeding as he kisses our cheek.

It's not like I didn't warn him.

I met my rebound guy soon after a painful break-up. He owned his home, had a college degree, made good money. He was tall with strong arms. He made me laugh, not cry. He was there when he said he would be.

I let him in.

We quickly became lovers. We spent an amazing time in bed together. Out of bed, he was sweet, loving, and dependable. All new to me.

Did I fall in love? Did he? I don't know either of us could say we did. We *loved* each other, sure. (He could cook. I loved that.)

We didn't talk of the future — I was about ten years younger and eager to leave Sacramento; he'd been burned before (two broken engagements) and unwilling to go anywhere.

Neither of us wanted to go *there*.

That became an easy passport to hang onto for a while. No expectations meant no angst.

One night, I came over and the house was dark, save a candle with a note and a blindfold. "Put this on. No questions." This was new. His place was rockin' to a house beat, slammin' so loud I couldn't think. Soon his hands were on me, stripping me slowly. My heart raced, every nerve on edge for the next moment.

I didn't know what he had planned, and if you've ever let yourself be blindfolded in a sexual situation, that's where the trust comes in.

It's a test. It was the first time I'd been blindfolded. It's clear he had a whole *9 & 1/2 Weeks* kind of thing planned for me, for us.

And I went along with it. I got into the zone.

For a while.

And then I didn't.

I can't recall exactly the moment I freaked, but I did. The feeling of claustrophobia so intensely strong, I ripped off the blindfold, grabbed my clothes, ran to his bathroom.

Then *he* freaked, unable to comprehend why I couldn't, wouldn't trust him.

You know I'd never hurt you.

I cried. I did trust him. He couldn't have been more gently sensual with me, knowing it was my first time in this situation. Sure, he was enjoying himself; but he also wanted to share something hot between us. Something that was only, truly ours.

Did I trust him? Yes. So where did this feeling of claustrophobia come from?

I think our subconscious dictates to us in situations where we have no conscious thought, comprehending for us. Suppression, repression. I didn't immediately understand. In fact, it took me months to realize it was my college date rape experience that made my fight-or-flight response kick in.

But as I cried in his bathroom, I couldn't verbalize this. My problem-solving skills were nil as I pulled on his t-shirt and crawled into his bed, covers up to my neck with confusion and guilt, while he massaged me and watched Conan.

One day soon after, I woke up, watching him sleeping at peace next to me, and decided I didn't see us together in sixty years.

That was it. I was done. The rebound guy had done his job.

What!? He responded with incredulity. *How can you possibly know that?*

I allowed him to put me back together again in his own way.

I made him bleed.

The rules for the rebound guy are simple: expect to receive what you've fixed.

A heart for a heart.

Everybody knows that.

I NEED A LOVER

I loved him.

My heart bled when he left.

I cried on my floor for months, going about my days in a bewildered stupor.

Then, suddenly, I was done. I got up, disgusted with myself. Who was he to take away my passion for life? Who was I to let him?

Then I got pissed at the cheating bastard.

My best friend J by my side, telling me he wasn't worth it, I reentered the world.

Then I met Rebound Guy (see last essay).

He was a healthy guy who rarely drank, never did drugs, college degree, and all the rest. I told myself I wanted a guy who had all that, and here was this guy who had all that, so he must be The One.

Physically, no question, he was my ideal. Tall, muscular, fit. I'd always been attracted to tall, big men; I liked the physicality of a man around me, given my small stature. M fit the bill. After my massive hurt, Rebound Guy covered me. He made me feel safe.

He was shy. Sweet. Though we started slowly, we progressed quickly. It wasn't long before he had me in his bed, lovingly holding me close after making love. He cared for me, and I embraced the good.

Then came the bad. He started negatively commenting on my body, watching every bite of food I took. He started insisting that I look like the girls in the *Playboy* magazines I found that he had collected since high school. The magazines themselves? Not a problem with me. His unrealistic expectation that I look like the women in them with their size 1 or 3 unhealthy bodies, large breasts (clearly fake), dark tans, and plastic looking? Definitely a problem, but one I put up with for far too long.

No more than 105 pounds at the time, I didn't understand his criticism and started wondering, *am I fat?* Hanging out in my bikini, tanning in his backyard in the summer, watching every morsel of food that entered my mouth already, did he want me to crash diet? Get lipo? A boob job?

Yes, yes, and yes.

He started me on an exercise regimen and even a diet, neither of which were bad for me, per se. Protein shakes, eat half of any food. Dessert? God, no. I didn't see any harm in it; he was a good boyfriend, caring, loving. *He only wants what's best for me, right?*

Once, his older brother came over while I was hanging out in my bathing suit. His brother said I was hot. My boyfriend said I would be, as soon as I lost ten pounds.

The danger of being a twenty-something woman and having a man telling you that you are fat is the damage it does to your self-esteem. An obvious statement, right? One would think.

Yet, here I was. Physically fit from years of jogging and gymnastics, with a guy who told me regularly I was fat. Someone who supposedly loved me. Who never said it in a mean way, but in a way that made me feel I would be that much prettier, more desirable, if only I'd lose that extra weight, get those fake boobs, do lipo. Who *could* be perfect. If only.

What a brainfuck.

He must have thought he could make me, his imperfect possibility, into his perfect reality.

Then I left him. The day I woke up and broke up with him seemed sudden, but I think all his comments had built up and I reached a point where I wanted to take me back. I didn't want to belong to anyone but myself.

His conditioning stayed with me and affected my eating habits. It took me YEARS to take a bite of food without feeling guilty. Even an apple (sugar, bad). I only ate half of everything and spent *years* hungry.

Our subconscious remembers what we willingly shove aside. It can take years to undo damage to our self-esteem. And guess what? I don't blame him.

I blame myself. I take responsibility for allowing him to affect me. He wanted what he wanted, and I allowed his desires to become a part of me. Being vulnerable isn't always a bad thing. Sometimes it is.

The woman I am today? She would never allow something like that to happen. No way. If I saw that manipulation, intentional or not, I'd be out of there.

As a woman who has now experienced two pregnancies, and the inherent weight-gain that comes with them, I'm grateful to have a man next to me who loves me no matter what. Who tells me I'm beautiful. Who doesn't want a "weekend pass" with his dream girl, since he says he gets that every weekend.

He has never made me feel bad about my body. Ever. And if he did? I wouldn't be with him anymore.

A Threat Is A Threat

"If you say anything about my sleeping with Karen to Jane *I will kill you*," a male colleague said to me one day.

I was at work. In my office. In the home office of a large company.

I thought we were friends, pals. I'd invited him to my wedding, for God's sake.

Was he serious? No. He surely must be joking, right?

Apparently not, because he repeated his threat.

Well over six-feet two and two hundred pounds, he glared down at me as I sat in my office chair, terrified. Standing over me he said it again, pointing for emphasis.

Then he left, slamming my door.

Trembling, I called my new husband and told him what happened. He wanted me to call the police.

Instead, I went my manager, who advised me to shut up.

"Surely he wasn't serious. He's so funny and charming. Always joking. I'm sure you just misunderstood him, Rachel." She scolded me in her manipulative Southern drawl, more affected when she wanted to make a point, looking me directly in the eye to be sure I understood her loud and clear.

(Months later, when I went to her for help dealing with a male superior who made crude, sexual comments to me in front of a class of trainees, she told me I should feel flattered that I was "cute enough" for him to make those comments to.)

Disappointed with her reaction, I went to HR. Surely Human Resources will back me, I thought hopefully. They wrote down everything I said as I relayed the exchange and the death threat. When I was done, both the male and female HR managers put down their pens and advised me to work it out directly with him.

Yes, they put the onus on me to fix this "misunderstanding."

So let's see if I have this straight: the guy is sleeping with two women in our department, telling me bits and pieces about his sexcapades, and when I asked him to stop sharing with me, he loses his shit, threatens to kill me, and *I've done something wrong?*

Yeah, and I must have worn the wrong thing that day, too.

Sure, I guess because I allowed him to confide in me in the first place, it's my fault. 'Cause I should know what's coming out of a total stranger's mouth. Yup.

And sure, I should know he has a history of sleeping with colleagues (well, anyone really) since I was the new kid and had only been at my new position with this branch for just a few days when they placed him with me *as my mentor.*

HR's suggestion: we go on a business trip together. As if that would fix everything.

I told my boss NO WAY. And because I refused, it went in my file that I was being — what's the word? Insubordinate.

Sadly, this kind of lightheartedness about a threatening situation isn't all that uncommon.

Even today, more than twenty years later, I still shake my head in sympathy for the young woman I was, the girl who didn't know the rules. I had thought there were departments in place to protect from that kind of thing, but I was let down by the very people who should have helped me. And I did nothing more.

What would I do differently now? Call the police. No question. Someone threatens to kill you —at all, let alone twice — you fucking well call the cops. A threat is a threat. And it requires no apologies on the victim's part.

FLY

No way to hide, I let you in.
Pervading my dreams, you fill my body.
Desire drips
At the mere touch
of your voice.

Instant bond nurtures.
Your body speaks words.
Your eyes fasten on
My heart.

Feeling
A rip,
The universe shifts
To borrow
A place
To fly.

A DOUBLE-SPACED LIFE

Rest, baby.

Dream.

As you say that, I realize, no. I can't.

I don't know what it's like to rest.

To not work.

To not write.

To not drive.

I thought I did.

Once.

I gave myself over to a man.

Luxuriating in the grasp of his astonishing love. Carrying my fears on his broad shoulders, I let his dreams be enough to stretch my soul.

Praying to be still.

But a lover's arms cannot replace the secret inside your soul, one you must let out or it will rip across your double-spaced life. Threatening your very being, you might explode and run screaming, naked, down a crowded street —

And then everyone will know.

So I work.

I write.

And I drive.

For me. For us.

For our double-spaced life.

SNAP

She watches his growing silence with curiosity and wonder. So still, waiting to feel his words she knows will come.

Like they will. Like they always do.

Never knowing what she's done, walking that fine line only he can see, a tightrope of triggers snapping at any moment. His dam of emotion walled up tightly, one single step causes a flood that leaves her drowning in numbness for days.

This time: A study date. All it takes to break the rope.

He knows she can't control another, even though she's tried so hard. She knows she can't control that. She has also learned it's a long, lonely walk from trying to knowing.

Yet still — she hears his pain, touches his fears. His feelings for her so strong, he staggers beneath their weight.

The air changes. She notices the crack in the silent lull right before she feels the first sting.

Knowing it's meant with love.

After, he pins her to the bed and fucks her. No preamble, he roughly spreads her legs open, thrusts deep. His hardness hurts her. One hand shoves her head to the side so he won't see what he perceives as her betrayal.

Punishing.

The crowded tunnel seethes with pain, love, fear, sex — their intensity a wild craving she never knew existed, one she isn't hungry for but now, can't seem to get enough of. She does not see light, isn't sure she's even looking for it.

Who surrenders to this madness? Who has she become?

Loving, sweet, he tends to her later. Eyes on hers, he claims her tears. Pressing her bruises, he smiles that knowing smile pulled out only for her.

Hungering for *this* attention, she inhales his feral scent created just for her. He soothes her with words she can't feel through the pain she can't hear. Curiosity and wonder are deadened by her silence.

She knows who she has become.

TEARS OF BLOOD

I am in pain. I feel as if my skin has shards that bleed when anyone touches me.

"Touching me will only hurt you," I tell my babbling baby sister, as I gently push her hand away from my wet face. I wonder if my tears are made of blood.

The desperation brimming. Maybe ending my life is my only option.

I will be twelve next week.

Living in my own mad world I was supposed to feel the way that every child should. Grasping for normalcy, yet I dreamt for it all to end.

I didn't understand why he chose me. I was just a little girl. I knew his touching me was wrong. I knew I should tell. But ... but if I did, he would kill me. He told me so. He showed me his gun. The weight of it so heavy. He would kill my parents, my beloved baby sister.

As I hold her pudgy little legs, squeezing their soft skin, I can't bear it. I'm wearing my Raggedy Ann pj's as I sit crying, rocking her. Nobody sees. Nobody asks. She reaches for my tears with her jerky baby movements.

It's all mixed up in my head. If I take some of my mom's pills and just end it, nobody will ever know what happened. He won't touch me anymore. Nobody will know how my skin crawls, those words he said, my shame. He can't come after me for telling. I can save my family.

He stares at me every day.

Then comes the sheriffs, courts, testifying, sentencing, prison.

And the years go by.

He comes back gray. I am older. I am angry.

He still stares at me every day, hatred burning in his eyes.

I'm still stuck. I'm in high school. I have nowhere to go. I see boys. I get high. I tell nobody what happened, but I wonder: who does that to a young girl? I know more now about men and their needs. I've got curves. I understand *that*.

I also understand there are sick fucks in this world. I know going to jail didn't make him less of one. Every time he looks at me I wonder if the boys will see what he did to me. My face burns with the stigma of one who knows what it means to carry a red-lettered burden.

When he dies, I feel nothing. No victory, no forgiveness, no tears. His blood no longer flowing should assuage my pain, but all I feel is cold finality.

His death, my breath.

HOME

You came to me.

I didn't invite you in. Yet here you are, nestled inside my heart.

Craving your touch.

You told me to look away, but there was never a chance of that once you singed my skin with your eyes.

Burning for you.

Cells created just for you, reassuring me I have no control of the needs inside me reach out in the darkest recesses of this violet night of revelation.

Holding me as if we were meant to fit.

If you need me, I am here with my door open. I have no choice.

I hear your call before you make it. I know your soul as you know mine. Like the plaintive howl of a single guitar string, I cry for what you do to me.

I fear a life without you and wonder how I'll go on without your fire inside me.

Burning for you.

Take me home, Love.

Make me home, Love.

A Letter To A Former Lover About Falling

You killed yourself three years ago.

Atoms that occupied your space split and fell.

Fall. The word has many meanings.

At lunch we spoke. At dinner, you were gone.

Grief is an interesting emotion, in that everyone handles it differently. I immediately became so angry at you, for being so incredibly selfish. For many years, I still held you in my heart.

How dare you break it again? You had no fucking right.

Selfish bastard.

When you visit in my dreams, you're always out of reach, but calm and happy. These dreams are a message from the universe that your atoms haven't fallen.

They've simply reorganized — now another meaning for fall.

CROSSING THE RIVER

The river is wide and oh, so deep, and it winds and winds around. I dream we're happy in my sleep, floating down and down and down

— "Riverwide," Sheryl Crow

Bright red blood on his white shirt.

A baseball bat he kept behind the seat of his ridiculously tall white truck.

What I remember about my first time.

Not sex, though God knows we left our moist skin all over that long vinyl bench seat.

No, this was my first time witnessing a man go to unprecedented violent lengths.

My man erupted powerfully into a glaze-eyed stranger.

Who was this strange, violent man in front me?

He was from a foreign land where men used their fists. Their favorite choice of weapon to make their point loud and clear? Something that made a clean crack.

It was a fight over a parking spot.

To him, it was territorial pride. His steely desire to give me everything, whether it was his to give or not. The point? To him, he couldn't make it without showing people the violence he was capable of.

Youth? Ego? Protectiveness?

I still can't wrap my mind around crossing that line of human behavior — civilized people punching and fighting, making violence their communication of choice.

Is it because I'm a woman, I've never considered hitting someone who acted inappropriately? Even one of my best male friends, a gentle man, a believer in spirit and mankind, has thrown a few punches in his time.

As a writer, my weapons are words. The thought of hurting someone physically to prove my point has never and will never be an option for me. Well, let me amend that: if someone hurt my child in front of me, tiger-mother's claws would come out.

He could be very loving with me. Sweet, tender, every bit the gentleman. And yet, I feared his violent side. I instinctively knew, no. This is not right. *For me.* But the intensity of his "good" behavior overcame all rational thought; so I stayed.

Is it a mistake of youth to fall for the bad boy? I'm glad I experienced him, us, even myself in this situation. The Law of Attraction states *'like attracts like,'* — so what did that make us? Not a violent person, I didn't *like* his violence. I abhorred it. But I unknowingly *loved* the intensity of him.

What to do?

Once I believed in things unseen; I was blinded by the dark. Out of the multitude to me, he came and broke my heart.

Didn't matter. He ripped me apart by cheating. Taking him back was my mistake. My trust for him splattered like drops of blood. After he cheated again, I left.

We were not unique. Were we different than many young couples in their early twenties? I'd ask myself then. I realize now the wrecked reality I lived with him, wanting more until he wanted too much of me.

Tell ma I loved a man, even though I turned and ran. Lovely and fine I could have been, laying down in the palm of his hand, laying down in the palm of his hand, staying down in the palm of his hand.

No regrets or worries about wasted time. I'd have to blame myself for loving and learning. Experiencing this craziness and coming out of it fairly unscathed is a shiny gem I carry in my pocket.

When I crossed the river, I left him standing alone on its sparkling edge.

BAD BOY THEORY

There's no reason for it to have happened. I certainly knew better.

But there I was: young, in love.

At least once in her life, a girl will fall for the wrong guy. The bad seed. The bastard. The rebel.

Here's my theory as to why. This is important for our growth as women so we know how to be treated like shit. Yes, you read that right. Because, if any of our future lovers even *think* about such shoddy treatment, if even a flicker of violence or disdain crosses their brainstem, we'll kick their ass.

Or at least walk out with our dignity intact.

But when we're young, we take it. We think cheating and emotional distance are what we deserve. We bring what we wring.

So many evenings I struggled to fit into his mold. Caring girlfriend, sexy whore, future wife. All the things I thought he wanted me to be.

Until that one night —

When he brought home all the meth.

Mid-80s, he called it crank. I'd smoked pot since junior high. Tried coke. But this? This scared me.

Me: Why so much?

Him: I'm dealing now.

Me: What?

So fast, I don't see it coming; he slaps the shock off my face.

He'd never hit me before.

Oh, God, I'm sorry, babe. Don't look at me like that. I'm doing this for you, for us, he says as he shows me the gun.

I'm holding my stinging cheek, trying to process it all, as the doorbell rings. He stows the gun in the back of his pants, his finger to his lips, *Shhhhh.*

The house fills with men. Music, beer, his hand on my ass. *You're mine,* he whispers, his eyes glazed from the drugs.

I gotta go, I say, walking back into the bedroom to grab my purse. *Too much for me.*

He drags me roughly into his room and ties me to his bedpost, his shirt sleeves knotted tightly around my wrists. *You're mine,* he tells me with a feral, teeth-baring grin. *Don't ever fucking forget it.*

Ripping off my skirt, he grabs me roughly. *Don't. Move.* He warns me as he removes his pants, hard and ready.

Shoving into me, I gasp as I feel tender skin tear. He attacks my body. He's a stranger, wild-eyed, clutching and scratching my skin, leaving bruises that will last long after they fade from dark to light.

Pulling my hair back, he growls. I think I'm going to pass out, my heart races. *I can't breathe,* I cry.

He works hard, but can't get there. *It's the fucking drugs,* I say.

He stops.

His face, red and swollen, shows how angry he is with me because I couldn't make it happen. He sits on the bed with his hand to his head, as if to shake out the confusion filling his mind.

In that moment, I want to comfort him as much as I want to be freed.

That's where the bad boy gets you — the duality of your emotions worse than the shame.

He leaves me there, tied to the bed. Afraid another drug head might steal me away. His way of protecting his sopping, crying property.

I spend the night tied to him by our wrists, never giving in to sleep. We fuck, me wanting it now, knowing it would be the last.

I knew love shouldn't hurt. But it did.

It did.

I saw the reason as I walked out the door; the only thing I knew for certain.

This was not love, but a cruel bastardization of it.

THE ONE

Lots of people ask: "How do you know when you've found The One?"

I can only speak of my own experience, such a confluence of events that brought my husband and me together.

I met JP just three weeks after I'd moved across the country for a job promotion. I came alone, knowing nobody. I just knew I had to leave my hometown to grow and learn. I figured moving across the country alone would definitely help me do that.

On one of my first days on the job, my manager scheduled me for a training session required for all new members of the department. No big deal to me; I'd already been through so much training with this company, what was one more?

And yet, the people in my department were all aflutter. One of my coworkers mentioned her crush on the trainer of the session. So I wanted to see the deal with this guy. Why the big deal?

When we met, I was simply myself. I figured my friend had her sights set on him, and this was job training.

And yet, every time I looked up during the next day or so, his eyes met mine. When he asked at lunch if my husband and kids minded the move across the country, I threw him a bone: single, dude.

At a break from one of the sessions, my friend who supposedly had a crush on him told me she thought we would be cute together, and besides she'd just started dating a nice guy (whom she ended up marrying), so, she told me to do my thing. Did I have a thing? I liked him; he seemed normal from what I could tell. I gave him my card.

Which he promptly lost.

Fast forward a week and we have our first date. Wait, I have to back up one moment. This is the best part!

My eighty year old grandmother, Bamma, lived in Florida, kinda losing it and never, ever called me ; I always called her. But out of the blue she did. She told me she felt something big going on with me. I should also note that the date was February 5, my long-passed grandfather's (her husband's) birthday.

It was a short but incredibly portentous conversation. It's like the gods were watching over us. "I'm about to leave for a date, Bamma," I said. "Tell me about him," she said. I told her briefly as I didn't want to miss my train. I told her about his kind eyes.

"He's the one, darling," she said after I finished. "What? We haven't even gone on our first date!" I said, and made a mental note to tell my mom to call Bamma the next day to check on her.

I headed into the city on the train where I was to meet him at Grand Central. One of my coworkers, a very large, very big African-American guy, drove me to the station. "He touch you, you call me. Ya hear?" He said as he handed me his mobile number on a scrap of paper, ensuring I put it where I could find it with ease in my purse. "I don't care what time it is, you call." I agreed. He was a good guy. Very sweet, actually.

JP promised he'd meet me at the station, right on the platform. I exited and no JP. I didn't know NYC at all, or the trains, or the station. But I stayed calm, walked slowly toward the exit. And there he stood. With a rose and a CD.

Sweet. Okay, corny but sweet.

We went to FAO Schwartz. I know, not normal first date kind of fare, but because my niece would be celebrating her birthday the next week, I really wanted to buy her something cool. And I did (I think. I really can't remember what I bought. I lost everything outside of JP).

From there we had an amazing dinner in the Village, took in a Broadway show (*The Secret Garden,* my favorite book ever — I had mentioned it. He remembered and bought tickets for this show for that reason. I know. Smooth.), and drinks afterward at the Tavern On The Green Bar.

By then we'd gotten quite cozy and made out like a ship going down (my husband's favorite line about the night).

Then he called me a car and off I went. To my little townhouse in New Jersey. Alone. Neither of us wanted this date to end, but it was time. We recognized, I think, even in those early moments, that we had a future. We wanted to wait.

The next date, however, sealed the deal.

Within one month, he told me he loved me. *Me: How is that possible? Him: Not the answer I expected, but okay,"* he said and launched into all the reasons. I was overwhelmed, excited, a little scared.

Could he be The One? Did I know? Could I know?

When he asked me to marry him two months later, I said …

Yes. Without hesitation. Yes.

STALKING ISN'T A PLOT POINT WHEN IT'S REAL

Stalking: to proceed in a steady, deliberate, or sinister manner.

As a woman somewhat in the public eye, I've had my share of stalkers. Some are social media trolls I want to believe are truly harmless: they tell me I'm pretty or taunt me, ask a few questions that are much too personal (which I don't respond to). I block them, and that, as they say, is that. However, a few have crossed that invisible line of merely annoying to threatening.

In my case, my stalkers have been men. (Most [78%] stalking victims are female and most [87%] stalking perpetrators are male.*)

Three very good female friends of mine have been stalked. One repeatedly, for many years, by a young woman. The other two, by men. In all cases, the offenders were delusional — clearly, mentally ill. Which makes sense: Why would a completely healthy person stalk someone?

A few things I've learned with my experiences: never, ever engage personally with someone who is stalking you. When I filed my first police report, the sheriff told me that. The stalker's goal is to be part of your life, and the biggest payout is attention from you, no matter if it's positive or negative.

The most terrifying part, for me, of being stalked is when I was placed in a situation with the stalker. I guested on a popular writing radio show, and he *called in*. The host put him on the air with me. I knew it was him the moment he stated his name and discussed the blog post I wrote that upset him so. I became mute. My heart raced. To hear his voice — in a situation that had nothing at all to do with him — totally surreal.

I followed the direction of the police. Despite his repeated attempts to engage me on social media, on my blog, on the radio, and perhaps, even in real life, I never once intentionally interacted with him.

However, I didn't hide. I still wrote my books and blog posts (which he objected to), and included the most controversial material, as I would have anyway. I refused to live in fear of what he would think or do. I blocked him everywhere I possibly could and he eventually went away.

Where do we draw the line between doing nothing and doing something? How do we take action against someone not in his or her right mind?

Is stalking a form of violent invasion? Dear God, yes.

I don't have all the answers. I can only share with you what I did. Anyone can be stalked, public figure or not. And with social media, people can easily and anonymously hide behind their monitors, which allows for voyeurism of a different kind. But stalking isn't always anonymous; they usually want to be known and that's what makes it terrifying.

I'm not a victim of stalking because *I'm not a victim*. Period. But there is a fine line between not engaging and not hiding. Each person must decide what the best course of action is to ensure their safety from those around them who are threats.

Stalking isn't a plot point when it's real. For me, there is NO gray area when it comes to this. Stalking is violent, it's threatening, and yet you can choose to not be a victim of it, even if you've been victimized. That's what I did. And no, it wasn't easy. I'm not saying it is. But it is possible.

While women are significantly more likely to be stalked by a male (sixty-seven percent) than a female (twenty-four percent), men are just as likely to be stalked by another male (forty-one percent) than a female (forty-three percent) – Source, RAINN.

UNDERWATER

He is afraid of losing his freedom.

She is afraid of capturing it.

Floating down a winding river, life came at them in unplanned, foggy waves of time.

Hazy days of tangled limbs and hushed breaths held too long, they hid splashes of love for each other like presents left in small pockets, forgotten in the rushing tide.

A quiet love, one that didn't throw, hurl, or hurt. A balm to her wounded soul, she gave him what she had been missing.

He feared it, this freedom, too much. He feared diving in more than cautiously watching from the edge.

The cool water runs over her skin; she welcomes the chill as she passes his wanting eyes.

And then she knows.

She'd found his hollow, the place he saves for rainy days, too small for both of them to fit. An abandoned, empty box she fills with tears.

His gift to her.

FLY AWAY

She tells him no.

Fly away. I can't do this.

He looks at her with those eyes. 'I don't want to be that guy, but I can't lose ...'

You're not. I'm that girl, though. I know and accept that.

He looks at her intently. 'The world will cave. Cracks will show. We may fall.'

I want this. I want you. Whatever it takes.

His hands shake, as if the words are struggling to come out of his skin.

She grabs his hands as if to say, I know.

I have to go. It's time.

He looks up, his heartbreak creating ruptured lines with every step she takes.

'Don't, baby.'

She stops at the doorway. *I'm just one woman.*

He takes a step, gets down on one knee.

She can't. She runs to her car. Away from the unknown, back to the nest.

'This isn't over! You are that girl!'

You cannot lose what doesn't want to be found.

She leaves him there, her future pounding in her heart as she drives away.

Flies away.

THE TASTE OF LONGING

It's not like I can wake up and wish you gone.

You're inside me now.

The words that billowed from your heart cannot be gathered and pushed back in.

I feel your passion and desire, waiting for the dance that never happens.

At least, not yet.

Like a butterfly in glass, I want to fly away to you but the invisible walls contain me. It's not time.

Hard to accept when I feel your words calling to me.

Your soul beckoning me with its pull.

Come to me, you say in one breath; stay, you say in another.

I taste your lips on mine and pray I make my way to you

As a butterfly chases its freedom.

So will I.

PURE WILL

"If you put your mind to it, you can do anything." A clichéd old adage, but it's a saying because it's true.

At age nine, I saw a female student, Susie, doing backflips across the backfield. I tried and landed on my head. But I was determined: *I am going to do that.*

I bugged my parents incessantly until they put me in the same studio as Susie. She was way beyond my skill level and we weren't really friends, but she welcomed me and showed me around.

Within three months, I did back handsprings, backs, aerials, and all other forms of tumbling. I was a flipper and I loved it. Every time I did a death roll (forward somersault with my head to the side), my mom would freak and beg me to quit.

Any spare expanse of grass or even dirt became my playground. I practiced day and night. Even in my sleep, where I tumbled in dreamland.

However, I hated the beam — it terrified me. The parallel bars hurt my hip bones horribly. I went over the vault and landed on my back — I couldn't move, scared I had broken my back or neck, or would be paralyzed. No, just sprained everything in my entire body. Even my eyelashes hurt.

In other words, I sucked at everything else. I only had the drive and desire for tumbling.

So, what to do?

My coach, Kay (God love her), did not respect the fear. "Do it, Goddammit!" she'd yell at me when I stood on the beam, shivering, afraid to do a backflip. She did not take my NO for an answer; no time for coddling with Kay.

Instead, she took me into the Class 1 (Class 3 was the newbie level) so I could train with the serious, competitive gymnasts. I stood in line as I watched each elite girl (and one guy, Todd. Isn't there always a

Todd?) follow Kay's directions: take *one* step and do an aerial (no hands), cartwheel or front walkover.

Um, sorry. What?

No running start? No round off? Surely this woman was crazy.

But guess what? *I did it.* I told myself I could do it, and I totally did. I told myself I could, took a step, and felt my body lift as if by magic.

It wasn't magic, though. It was pure will.

See, Kay knew something I didn't. Despite my fears, I had it in me to succeed at any challenge she gave me. Easily able but perhaps not ready... I just needed a push.

That moment helped define me as a person. It's still crystal clear in my head. The red mat, the hugs of congrats, but most of all, me standing there knowing *I did it.*

Having that kind of moment is part of what kept me going when the next year, our neighbor started to molest me. Though I was terrified — of him, of what he was doing to me — I knew I'd make it out the other side.

THE GRAY

I feel it closing in.

The blue sky untouchable. I reach my arm up as far as I can, but it's not enough. I know tomorrow my shoulder will ache from my effort, but I don't want to go to sleep without pushing some of the soft clouds away.

I need to see the sun.

Depression is something I never knew about first-hand until adulthood. I've written about how anxious and terrified I became after the birth of my first child, my girl, and how the thought of leaving her with a sitter propelled me into a non-functioning, crying mess.

I've discussed the molestation I experienced as a young girl.

What I haven't discussed is that though my daughter's now thirteen and a middle-schooler, I continue to take antidepressants. I still have anxiety when my kids are away from me, or my husband has to go out of town. If I can't find my phone, I freak — because how will someone let me know if everyone is okay if I don't have my phone right next to me, even in my sleep.

It's difficult living away from any friends or family, though I've done it successfully for gosh, over twenty-something years now. I am, as they say, quite independent. Now that we have moved back to my hometown, which I never thought I'd do, I feel a sense of peace.

Silence is one of the worst, most vocal enemies, yet people go through many bouts of depression, not sharing what is happening. People don't understand that, but as someone who suffers from it, I can tell you that it's difficult to be objective about the gray.

I described depression to my therapist as a misty fog that surrounds me, heavy on my shoulders, pervading everything and nothing at all. I liken depression to a bird stealing into the depths of your soul, pecking at your disposition until nothing is left.

And that is when you break into pieces.

I have no shame about it. I tried diet and exercise, everyone's answer. I've read a ton about it and I'd rather take the meds than be a nonfunctional mess. Chemical imbalances cannot be cured by vitamins and a positive attitude (sorry, Tom Cruise).

I have dosed down to see how I'd do, but the gray starts to close in again.

I've also observed the same phenomenon in my own family. My girl suffers from panic attacks and, making the necessary dietary changes and increasing her vitamins and exercise made no difference. I've come to understand that the potent mixture of chemicals and hormones play havoc with people, women especially.

I'll never forget when I reached out to my OB/GYN after I gave birth to my little girl over thirteen years ago, when I couldn't stop crying; when the anxiety took hold of my heart and squeezed so tightly I couldn't breathe. She told me that women are particularly susceptible to hormone imbalances and what I was going through wasn't unique. It even had a name: postpartum depression.

Knowing that made me feel better, and yet, worse. Better: knowing I wasn't alone in this helped immensely. She put me on Prozac that day and sent me to a terrific therapist. Within a few days, I started to feel normal, a sense of relief rolling over me in waves. Worse: why me? I don't mean to sound whiny, but wasn't it enough to feel like an alien for nine months, receive this beautiful, tiny gift that cries and rarely sleeps, while still feeling like the Michelin Man; now I had to add this?

The fog lifted and I could see where I was going once again. I even sat for a tattoo of a sun symbol inked onto my inner left wrist to remind me to look toward the light.

I've lost friends and a former lover to suicide. I know without a doubt that, had they reached out as I did, and asked someone, *anyone* for help, they would still be with us today.

Life is hard, but living it doesn't have to be.

RETURN TO ME

I lay my head down on a table of grief,
The rain of loss too heavy to bear.
Aching to hear your voice on my throat just once more.
Logic says you've left me,
As comprehension searches for unwanted truth.

Your scent lingers along my skin
Warming all I touch.
Your fire that used to soothe me on these cold, cold nights
Wraps around me in waves of heat before
Releasing me to the fall.

Too soon, too hot, too much,
Tangled guilt driving your head.
While your passion fills me,
Woven threads between our hearts,
Snap in your wake.

Desire, all I have left,
Lost inside your whispers.
Your voice a balm to my soul,
I pray you'll feel the silent pull
As I call you home.

Craving your touch,
I cry with your choice.

Distance may take me away,
Yet knowing it doesn't have to,
Makes this long night burn a slow flame, deep where there is no longer light.

I know that when the sun rises
So will I, from this table.

As dust turns to ash,
I accept the searing chill
Of what could have been
Branded on my swollen heart.

I remember your words, promises, and lies.

I only wish I'd known night would fall on our tomorrows.

A Letter To The Pedophile Next Door

Quite an experience to live in fear, isn't it? That's what it is to be a slave.

— Roy Batty, *Blade Runner*

(When my very good friend, author Gabe Berman, suggested I write this letter a while ago, I shrunk away and said no, not gonna happen.

But, here, in *Broken Pieces*, where I lay my soul bare, I decided: it's finally time.)

Dear Demon,

Twelve years old. Still a child. I collected Raggedy Ann dolls, loved gymnastics, and had just started to love writing.

Just twelve when you, the next-door neighbor to the left, extremely tall (at least six foot six) and big (over two-hundred something), set your sights on me.

After the first time, my world imploded. Everything I knew to be right about grownups as good and true traveled through my tainted blood, immediately making me feel like I didn't belong in a sane, normal world where people ate, drank, and slept. Where adults were either my teachers or parents, not men who invaded my body.

The cycle of becoming an adult quickly sped up; without my permission, clearly no longer a child. My life of innocence and trust ended, without any action on my part.

You gave the neighborhood kids scooter rides. We had fun, us kids. The parents figured their kids were safe since you were a responsible adult. Nobody else took that time with us. Parents mostly just wanted us out of their hair.

You took me to a secluded wooded area. You had a gun. I was twelve.

I told nobody, but I couldn't get through the day without crying, obsessed with the fear you would get to me again.

Which you did. Two or three more times.

I remember holding my then one-year-old baby sister, in my Raggedy Ann pajamas, and thinking I'd do *anything* to protect her from this shaming experience. I was not only a slave to fear, but to my every day existence.

I wanted nothing more than to roll into a tiny ball and hide under my bed. I would have done anything. Except tell. Because you had a gun. You were in the army. I knew you knew how to use it.

Eventually, it all came out. As one of the older children you molested, I could give a voice to what you did. There were trials. Yes, plural: a civil trial and then a military trial. It was as difficult as you would imagine it to be.

I remember what I wore the day the military car showed up in front of our house: black, boatneck, happy stripes. I was terrified, as if I had done something wrong. My life became too much of the unfamiliar. I remember having to sit in a courtroom and swear to tell the truth on a Bible, just like on TV. I remember going with my grandmother. My parents didn't want to hear.

I told a room full of adults how and what and where and when. They wanted to hear in great detail what you did. To me. To those other tiny little girls.

You got a few years in jail. You were court-martialed and lost your pension. Your wife descended into mental illness. Your kids and I avoided being in the same areas at school, knowing we had this unspeakable secret people just couldn't comprehend. That we, none of us, could comprehend. We were now bonded in a way that made no sense, members of a club nobody wants to ever be a part of.

I still felt ashamed.

My folks did the best they could. To this day, we don't talk about it. My mom has asked me exactly what happened but I don't see the need to go into the sordid details of your actions. I've been in therapy for a while and my shrink is very pragmatic — will it help to discuss the specifics? No. So, we don't.

We do discuss the far-reaching effects the experience has had on me. When I gave birth to my daughter thirteen years ago and I had to leave her with a sitter on my return to work that my world imploded — again. Though I couldn't verbalize it, I became terrified of leaving her alone.

Because of what you did; not just to me but to those precious, tiny little girls. Girls not much older than my own baby sister.

I do talk about the fact that it happened, not only because you've made it part of who I am now, but also because it can happen to anybody's children. Sure, times are different now and parents are more protective, yet we hear my story every day.

I don't live in fear, but I am very cautious about the people who are around my kids. Just one of your many gifts to me.

In my late twenties, you died. When my mom told me, my initial reaction: nothing. No happiness, no fear, nothing. Perhaps I was thankful that you were finally gone from this earth and could never hurt another child.

Thankful that you, Demon, are dust.

SINGED

Strip away all thoughts about us.

Close your eyes.

Tell me what you cherish.

Tell me what you love.

No more analysis, no more wondering, no more questions.

The answer is here floating around us, as if woven by silvery threads of silent certainty.

Look at me in the fading light, my hand over your heart.

What do you *feel*?

I don't want to hear about why we can't be together. About what's right or wrong. There will always be reasons why: shouldn't, couldn't, won't.

Do you want to always be wondering, 'Is she the one?' Will you regret not even trying? I see your struggle as your words march in rigid formation.

Stop.

Close your eyes.

Touch my heart.

Feel.

With your voice, I breathe fire. With your touch, I feel singed. With your scent, I feel lost.

Less than love doesn't exist for us.

Time moves both ways. I see our future and our past in your dark eyes as I wipe a tear from your darker fringe of lashes,

A drop of what? Could. Be.

Falling on my hand.

I walk to the window for a peek inside our souls.

I am yours, I cry.

Will you take my hand?

IT COULD HAVE BEEN WORSE

I recently hosted a few guest blogs by my friends Jessica Swift and Kelly Stone Gamble where they each relayed a terrifying experience and how they have dealt with it (stalking and kidnapping, respectively). Both are some of the strongest women I know and while I've never, thankfully, experienced those particular traumas, I understand one aspect very clearly: keeping it quiet. Not making a big deal.

Secrets are secrets for a reason.

While the trauma of my own childhood molestation remained a secret for much of my life, I feel I need to address one part of it that, besides the physical abuse, makes people uncomfortable: *talking about it*. Not only that, but the immediate reaction to downplay it: *well, it could have been worse*.

My folks were quick to downplay: "well, what the neighbor did to other, smaller children was much worse." It's our instinct to protect our own, and I'm sure my parents wanted to help me cope. But telling me and others that, while what happened to me was indeed truly awful, it could have been worse. He could have done a lot of other, even more horrible, sexual things to me. He could have killed me, or a member of my family. At least I was alive and didn't bear any physical scars.

Which is all true.

The problem with that way of thinking is that it diminishes and invalidates the feelings of the 'victim' of the crime (and it's not lost on me that I wrote that without saying 'my feelings'). I don't see myself as a victim, but the fact is, there is a purely objective definition to the word, which applies to this situation: the neighbor perpetrated a crime and chose me as his victim.

Awful, what happened to me. To others. Terrifying. An experience that brought a twelve-year-old girl to the brink of suicide from the shame of it all. Of course I didn't know or understand that at the time; that thinking about ways to die as an escape would be considered suicide. I understand what happened to me happened at a time when people didn't regularly go to therapy (mid-70s), and parents didn't worry about their kids in the overprotective way we do now.

I don't blame anyone. Most people who tried to comfort me either had never experienced it, didn't know what to say, or were embarrassed, understandably. Most safe twelve-year-old topics stick to Barbies or the latest pop song. People just didn't know what to do or say.

Nobody prepares you for how to deal with it, without special training, of course.

Part of being the victim of a crime is acknowledging that it happened. Owning that mantle that nobody would ever want. Understanding it's not shameful or my own fault.

Religion has never been a big thing for me. Too structured, too many foreign words I didn't understand. But I do believe in some kind of higher being who brings people and situations to us to learn and grow. Certainly it's helped me become an extraordinarily protective parent, very close to my kids, but still allowing them to thrive.

Nothing is easy in this life. If there's anything I've learned from this situation, it's that. And yes, bad stuff happens to good people, which sucks. Maybe we doubted we could rise above at some level, but we did. We all know these experiences happened for some unknowable reason. And sharing our stories can only help others.

As one blog commenter said, we are not victims. We are thrivers. If it had been worse, I may not be here today to write about it.

Believe me, for that I am eternally grateful.

INSIDE YOU

I'm no longer afraid of the dark.

I've been inside that clawing center of it, scratching away at the scarred insides of those entangled wires and climbing my way out. Yet some of those hours stay with me, no matter how much I try to excise them.

You touched me because you understood the tricky navigation of the murky waters inside me. Caressing me with your quiet words murmured in the still of that cloudless night, I relaxed into you, believing your talk of love.

As you pull away now, I let you go; safe in the knowledge you will return. The cruelest joke the universe gives us is thinking we can make up for lost time. Until then, we luxuriate in the shared, anguished longing of what we inevitably will be.

My world, created by glass and flame in the birth of your heat, implodes inside the shadowed walls of my heart.

I swallowed the shards you gave me, your eyes on mine.

Nothing is easy.

I wait, feeling your hands holding the shattered pieces of my soul together in the molten, darkest recesses of the heart you claimed, unwilling to give up.

I am inside you, waiting to come out.

BOOK CLUB QUESTIONS FOR *BROKEN PIECES*

1. For the person who chose *Broken Pieces*: What made you want to read it? What made you suggest it to the group for discussion? Did it live up to your expectations? Why or why not?

2. What do you think motivated Rachel to share her life story? How did you respond to her "voice"?

3. How did you feel reading this book? How has this book changed or enhanced your view of Rachel?

4. How does Rachel draw the reader in and keep them engaged? Does she convey her story with comedy, self-pity, empathy, or something else?

5. Were there any instances in which you felt Rachel was not being completely truthful? How did you react to these sections?

6. Is Rachel someone you would want to know or have as a friend in real life? If so, why?

7. Compare this book to other memoirs your group has read. Is it similar to any of them? Did you like it more or less than other books you've read? What do you think will be your lasting impression of the book?

8. What did you like or dislike about the book that hasn't been discussed already?

9. Rachel employs different techniques: poetry, prose, and essays, in a seemingly unordered manner. What was her intent in presenting the book in this style? Why do you feel she used this technique?

10. Were you glad you read this book? Would you recommend it to a friend? Do you want to read more works by Rachel?

ACKNOWLEDGMENTS

To my wonderful family: JP, Anya, and Lukas, who put up with my nights and weekends of writing, writing, always writing.

Mom and Dad, who support me no matter what I write.

My awesome editor and kindred, Jessica Swift Eldridge.

My other awesome editor and brother I never had, Justin Bog. Thanks for reading this before anyone else and being so lovingly honest.

Caren and Leslie, sisters extraordinaire.

Authors Kelly Stone Gamble and Gabe Berman for allowing me to mention them.

To my amazing betareaders, who I love both hearing and learning from.

And all the wonderful readers and authors who support and inspire me every day to write better. And then write even better than that.

Want to read more of my work?

A WALK IN THE SNARK

*"The Bait & Switch technique is illegal. Hmm. Correct me if I'm wrong…
but isn't that called…marriage?"*

INTRODUCTION TO "MEN VS. WOMEN, DECONSTRUCTED"

When I started writing the Mancode pieces, it was pretty easy, to be honest.
In my mind, it was about the goofy stuff guys do and how we chicks interpret them, and that interplay. Hard drives vs. sex drives. Our need for more shoes vs. their need for well, geek stuff from thinkgeek.com. Straightforward, right?

Turns out, not so much.

People talk about the Mancode in a lot of different ways.

There's the Maxim mag Mancode, the single guy's "if you date your best friend's ex-wife, don't tell him about it, you idiot," kind of thing; or "never sit right next to your best male friend in a movie theater" nonsense. Highbrow stuff.

Then there are a few very serious Mancode tomes out. And I mean, very serious. Like I was not aware it was an insult to my femininity if a guy walked on my right side. You know that gentlemen must always open doors for their ladies (which brings up a whole other problem… um… what if I'm not a lady), and watch girlie movies without complaint (so that's what guys are supposed to do—read the manual!). Duh!

Needless to say, my posts and tweets about men's—let's say "odd"—behavior, sparked quite a bit of debate, which rocked. I also received a lot of terrific feedback from men on my Twitter stream and blog, who asked me for some interpretation—why do chicks not say what we mean?

Men were confused. Is there a special code? Was there an AP class in high school they should have taken in order to understand women better? (Yeah, probably.) Why do women set their watches differently than men? Why do we speak in shoes?

So, I branched out into my series of Chickspeak pieces and "Deconstructed" articles, in the hopes that readers of all types—single, married, male, or female—could have further insights into our foreign-girl species.

That's about when the attorney cautioned me that people might use my book as legal advice; I figure that if someone rearranges the days of the week (See "Days of the Week, Deconstructed") after reading that section of the book, well, they probably need more help than I do, buddy. Please prove me right!

MEN ARE FROM *SEINFELD*, WOMEN ARE FROM *FRIENDS*

I was never that much of a believer in the whole *Men are from Mars, Women are from Venus* thing. My husband and I communicate fairly effectively...he brings me coffee in the morning and I say, "What took you so long?"

It works out just fine, thank you very much.

We've been married eighteen-plus years, and we've worked out most of the little "tube of toothpaste" things that drive most couples crazy. My guy came trained pretty well, I have to admit. He does his own laundry (more on that in a minute), he cooks (more on that, too), and he um...thinking...oh yeah, makes a killah martini.

However. Lately, there seem to be a few things that are driving me up the wall. And, based on some of my girlfriends and their comments about their men, I'm not alone.

Most men live by **The Mancode**. Even though they will *disagree* with you on this or even *defend* their actions, they have rationalized this guy stuff they do. If you are newly married and want to adorably defend your darling husband who does none of these things, you swear, go ahead.

Just wait, honey. He will.

Here are some examples:

- A MAN will drop his wet towel right NEXT to the hamper, on the floor. Why? Because it's wet. Oh, *of course*. That just makes *so* much sense. (Insert look of incredulity here.) Same goes for dirty socks and (ugh!) underwear.

- A MAN will be completely befuddled and unable to take the empty roll of toilet paper off the holder. He is physically incapable of putting the new one on. He wasn't able to do this as a boy, and it continues to be beyond his capabilities as a grown man. The same principle applies to the empty paper towel roll in the kitchen, by the way. He simply cannot do it. It's a DNA thing.

- A MAN is unable to use the deodorizing room spray that has been placed so thoughtfully by you in the bathroom for the sole purpose of covering up his stink after his use. He sees it, he knows how to use it; he just chooses not to. He revels in his stink. It's somewhat akin to a dog marking his territory. He thinks it was awfully nice of you to put it there as a decoration, though.

- Speaking of bodily functions, your MAN is so used to habitually farting and burping at a loud volume to "impress" you that he forgets to use his quiet fart/burp "voice" when company is over, particularly when the children's friends are visiting, resulting in crimson faces and tears of said children. "Oh, well," is his usual response, along with murmurs of something about being the king of the castle.

- A MAN will make as much noise as humanly possible when told to be quiet by an exhausted mother, especially if there is a colicky newborn in the house—or in my case, a testosterone-filled five-year-old Tasmanian devil child—who has just fallen asleep. When this poor, tired, bedraggled mother asks, begs, pleads with the daddy to please, please, *please* be quiet, just this once, the MAN will inadvertently bang shut every drawer, door, and window in sight. And then yelp loudly because he slammed his wittle, bitty finger, thus waking the sleeping babe. Goddamn it.

- A MAN will help around the house. He is a giver. He will even, at times, throw in a load of laundry. Where it will stay. Forever. Men do not fold clothes. Ever. Men do not put clothes away. Ever. It is written.

- A MAN *will* cook. (How do you think he wooed you in the first place?) Mine does. However, he will use every pot, plate, and utensil you've ever owned in the process. Your kitchen will look like the Battle of Gettysburg. He will, of course, be so exhausted by all this preparation (read: using all that stuff) that he can't possibly clean it all up. He will kindly leave that for you. Of course he will.

- A MAN will go to the grocery store as long as he has The List. Now, sending a MAN to the store is like sending him into a foreign country. Though he has been there a million times before, and has eaten the same brand of bread since birth, he must call you for confirmation before purchase, *or else he won't buy it.*

- You must be specific with The List, or he won't come home with the items you've requested. Write down SOUP and you're likely to get soups from China you didn't know existed, accompanied by explanations of "Well, I didn't know!" I can see you nodding.

- A MAN will listen to his TV programs at a volume that the people of China who actually made that soup can hear. If you do somehow manage to wrestle the remote away from his clutches to watch your own show, it is mandatory that he complain about the volume of your show (half of his), as well as the girliness of the content. It is written.

- A MAN can never find anything in the refrigerator without your help, even if it is right in front of him. This is called Refrigeratoritis in my home. It only strikes when I'm sitting down, finally, after a long day with the kids. Of course it does.

- Beware of letting your MAN drive your car. It will come back covered in receipts, food wrappers, sweatshirts, sundry bits of foreign matter, and with your cache of spare cash missing. Any thoughts you had of keeping your new car looking sparkling disappears like "tears in rain."

- Finally, a MAN will always take out the trash, but only after it is filled to overflowing, the puppy has decided to tear into it, and you've decided, damn it, that you will just do it yourself despite your bad shoulder and sore back. He will huff and puff and make a big deal out of it, but he will do it. He is doing YOU a favor, after all. It is singularly YOUR trash, you know.

The same concept applies to putting the large water bottle on the water cooler. The MAN will put it on but only when he's darned good and ready.

Now in all fairness, my husband is a good dude and takes my writing about these things in stride. He also makes a damn fine martini.

Of course he also said that he will be reading this post and commenting (when pigs fly).

So what does all this mean?

Easy…

Men are from *Seinfeld*. Women are from *Friends*.

"Men are from 'Do you want to do it tonight?'
Women are from 'Not if you ask me like that.'"

I'M TIRED, DECONSTRUCTED

Men are confused about stuff.

What kind of stuff?

Chick stuff.

No, not speaks quietly so as not to embarrass them *period* kind of stuff. Shhhh.

(Though of course *that* remains a mystery to most men and they will do anything AT ALL not to have to be anywhere near their women when blood is involved, especially when it comes to the actual drugstore buying of period paraphernalia.)

I know. The P word.

Run. Run away.

Honestly, men can be such babies.

But I digress.

No, what I wanted to talk about is simple, really.

Men seem to have little to no clue what we chicks mean when we utter this simple phrase: I'm tired.

Now, in all fairness, usually when we're tired — even though we are usually so exhausted that we are already asleep *before* we are already asleep — the phrase itself can mean *any number of things*.

Let me break it down for you, boys:

- You've decided to make your favorite stinky cheese garlic dish for *Monday Night Football* that nobody but you enjoys. You shop for it, you make it, you eat it. Then you leave the big ol' <u>mess</u> in the kitchen to be picked up; either by the magical cleanup fairy or someone else—clearly not your wife, who's looking at you sideways in a rather pensive manner, finger tapping on temple, trying to figure out where she set the sweet, caring, non-scented husband that she married.

- When you decide to GO FOR IT and wonder why you get the "I'm tired," guess what? SHE'S NOT TIRED! She's not even mad at you, really. She's more well, while repulsed is probably too strong a word, since hiding under that garlic blossom of a husband is the man she was attracted to enough to marry all those many, many, *many* years ago; let's just say she's more just um, biding her time until the Old Spice-smelling dude on a horse version she fell in love with shows up again.

  See…it's complicated.

- Add to that her disappointment that she's already cleaned the kitchen, even suppressing her gag reflex admiringly when it came to your pyramid-shaped, sort of *Close Encounters of the Third Kind*-looking heap of dirty toenail clippings left in a polite little mound on the dining room table. (Lucky for you she has a thing for Richard Dreyfuss.)

- Add that maybe she was hoping that while you were at the grocery store you might have remembered that not only was she was out of coffee, but also that the kids were out of their favorite fruity fruit snacks (since she not only asked you as you left, but also texted you. Twice.).

  Sigh.
  So, if you have not gotten it yet (eye roll), her "I'm tired" is kind of like a loaded gun.

- A further breakdown of what I'M TIRED really means, hip-hop style, if you will (insert chicka-chickah beat here and proceed):

  NOT NOW; I'M STILL MAD AT YOU FOR STEALING MY TIME-OF-THE-MONTH CHOCOLATE DONUT; YOU DIDN'T PUT DOWN THE TOILET SEAT AGAIN, AND SERIOUSLY, DUDE—ROOM SPRAY; WHY DIDN'T YOU PUT THE WINDSHIELD WASHER FLUID IN LIKE YOU SAID YOU WOULD, 'CAUSE OMG I CAN HARDLY SEE OUT THE TINY CIRCLE OF MY DIRTY CAR WINDOW; WHY IS THE DOG POOP STILL ON THE FRONT STEP, AND THEREFORE ON THE BOTTOM OF MY SHOES AND THEY ARE *PRADA*; AND YO, COULD YOU TAKE OUT THE TRASH THAT GOT PICKED UP, UM, YESTERDAY?

Listen, I'm the first to admit that women are complicated. Most men, on the other hand, are quite simple in their needs—and they will attest to that. If a guy says he's tired, he's usually tired.

And the reason he forgets stuff at the grocery store? Even with a list? 'Cause he's bought the chips and the beer. He's rushing home for one thing and one thing only.

That is, as long as he has Tivo'd the game.

My advice, fellas? Clean up the kitchen and for God's sake, put the seat down.

I guarantee our fatigue will magically disappear.

Kinda like that damn cleanup fairy.

"Imagine all the men, listening to what chicks say.
You may say I'm a dreamer. I'm clearly not the only one. #Mancode"

YOU LOOK FINE—LET'S GO

Do women wear makeup for ourselves, our men, or other women? Hell if I know. What I do know is that I'm not going anywhere without my lipstick and mascara…oh, and under eye concealer. Can't forget that.

Doesn't matter who's looking at me. I love makeup and it loves me. Or something.

Deal with it.

I may not look like Pat Benatar, but I can rock a red lip, damn it. Every chick has the right to play with her pots and potions.

Do not rush me. You will pay.

"*You look fine. Let's go.*" This is what my guy always says, tapping his foot impatiently as I put on my makeup...

But here's the thing.

I don't want to just look *fine*. I want to look great, wonderful, knock-his-socks-off fantastic.

Or, at least some days, good enough to fake it.

And I know that I can with a little help from my secret potions — mascara, lipstick, and concealer. If, given more time, eye shadow. Well, and eyeliner. And a little foundation. Oh, and some powder, too.

Hurry, somebody stop me...

My mother has never been much of a makeup wearer. She, like many women of the 50s, put on her lipstick, drew on her brows, and off she went into the world. Hello!

My older sister and I were lucky enough to be born with large eyes and long lashes — and no clue what to do with them. So what did we do? We did what all daughters everywhere do — went to our dad for advice. Huh?

Well, given that Dad was a manager for Longs Drugs, we soon had his fake-eyelashed cosmetician at our beck and call for personalized instruction — along with the cost plus ten percent discount on all makeup. Woo-hoo. (**First lesson: You don't pluck your brows — you pluck a chicken. You** *tweeze* **your brows.**)

After much trial and error (we really don't have to discuss that unfortunate lavender mascara, do we?), I've become adept over the years at putting on just enough to look like I'm not wearing any, or banging it out for a big night on the town.

I did have major lipstick anxiety when I found out I was pregnant the first time. My husband never seemed to mind getting lipstick on him — he liked knowing he'd been kissed. Yet I started to worry how on earth was I going to kiss my baby's precious cheeks (and soft tush and chubby legs and tiny toes) without covering them in goop?

This was most certainly not covered in the pregnancy bible *What to Expect When You're Expecting* — and I had the most updated edition.

Did being a new mother mean I had to give up lipstick?

Oh. My. God.

The husband just shook his head. He clearly didn't understand the seriousness of the situation. Men.

I'd ask my friends with new babies *not* "How was labor?" or "Is breastfeeding difficult?" but "How do you kiss her and not cover her in sticky gloss?"

I *really* needed to know.

But they were no help—they just wanted to talk about poop. Thankfully, my trusty Chanel came to the rescue. They make this fabulous Ultra Wear Lip Colour—I don't know what's in it, but I do know that it must have been created by NASA or something because it doesn't dry your lips out and the color stays on forever. It still looks good after kissing your guy or your baby—*and* after drinking martinis—always a plus.

Both of my men love it—the little guy calls it "magic lipstick" because I can sneak in kisses on his amazing cheeks and he doesn't get all goopy. The husband loves it because there's no taste—he hates glosses that have a taste (can't say I blame him) and it's the all-important "Can you put this in your pocket?" size slim.

If you are a guy reading this, go buy your chick one of these at Nordstrom or Saks— it retails for around $34—pricey yes, but so what? Think of all the kissing you can do and she won't be worrying about fixing her makeup. Plus, you get major points for actually knowing what Chanel is.

Of course, my honey still says I look great without all that "stuff." Mostly I think it's because he's just hungry and wants me to decide already <u>where we are going to eat</u>, damn it.

So I reply, "Thanks—that's so sweet. Now go away. I'm putting on my makeup."

MANCODE: EXPOSED

Is it possible to truly expose men?

Let me rephrase that.

Did it all start with Eve tempting Adam? Sure, if you believe in that stuff. (Hey, apples are good for you, man. Ask Benjamin Franklin.)

What this book is truly about: me, exposing my beliefs, experiences, and thoughts on men *and* women. Stripping off the pretense of stereotypes, undressing myself for your reading pleasure.

Okay, wait.

Mancode: Exposed has sex in it. If that offends you, move along. It's sarcastic and snarky. If your sensibilities run toward the conservative, you might not want to read any farther. (Pssst: I also throw in the occasional well-placed curse word or two.)

Men, women, sex, love, stereotypes. Important world topics like garages, lingerie, and um, chocolate? It's a melting pot (okay, now I'm just getting hungry).

But more than that, it's about all the levels in which we communicate… viewed through my looking glass of humor and deconstructed.

You can read the sections in this book in any order, though if you're starving, I don't suggest starting with Chocolate Confessions.

Anatomy and Physiology alone creates many fun predicaments— boobs and cocks are often subjects of humor because come on, that's just comedy gold. Someone says "Nuts!" and people laugh, right? Fair warning: this ain't your mama's biology class.

Coitus and Communication. We all do both. Some more, better, or worse than others. Many people lose their humor when it comes to communicating about sex, but I find that it's the connection between the two that fascinates me and for some reason, tends to bring out the snark.

Chocolate Confessions. Let's face it—chicks love chocolate. Men would be wise to understand that. We try to (Nutella) warn you. We've shown you our (Godiva) weakness. Honestly. Keep up.

DNA and Stereotypes. Possibly the most controversial section. I explore questions like, Can we outrun our DNA? Will we women always be slaves to our talkative nature (après sex)? Will you men never be free of the chains of your emotional withholding? Can we transfer man's paper towel changing abilities from garage to kitchen?

Read and see for yourself.

A few notes: You will see this sign # sprinkled throughout the book. Normally referred to as the number or pound sign (among other things) in the real world, it is called a hashtag (for metadata or searching) on Twitter. Words following hashtags are lumped together as one, so no, I didn't forget the spaces. It's a hashtag thing. Hashtags are such a great little shorthand tool, I not only speak in hashtags, I dream in them. It's sort of an addiction. Like staring at Brad Pitt's abs.

Also, I've chosen my most popular tweets to open each essay. These are the tweets that others have deemed their favorites over the past year and have retweeted or hit the "favorite" button multiple times. I hope you enjoy them also.

ANATOMY & PHYSIOLOGY

In this particular section, we talk bodies. If you're comfortable deconstructing things like the penis or vagina, I'm your girl. Hang out, stay awhile. Put on your Pradas and let's go, baby.

Women see a man scratching his stuff and want to run away. Quickly. Men see a woman rearranging her breasts, he's mesmerized. #imaginethat

I have this theory, based on too many martinis one night, that women speak in circles and men speak in points. (Hey, I'm a writer. I make shit up.)

Think about it.

When I tried to explain my whole concept to my guy, with the boobs and circles and penises and ...he cut me off and asked, "So, what's your point?"

I rest my case, your honor. #pointtaken

Welcome to the Anatomy and Physiology section. Men in all their um, glory?

You decide.

THAT'S 'CAUSE YOU DON'T HAVE A VAGINA

** *I'm a #snarky bitch. Tried to warn you. If you can't handle the snark, get out of the kitchen. I certainly did.* **

I think I've figured it out.

Part of this whole "*Men are from Seinfeld, Women are from Friends,*" thing.

I often say to my husband, when he can't figure out why I have to go get a pedicure or I'm going to DIE, "That's because you don't have a vagina."

Now unless you're a chick, a gay man, or well, Ryan Seacrest, you probably can't relate to that statement. However, any girl worth her weight in OPI's "I'm Really Not a Waitress" red knows exactly what I'm talking about.

Snap.

He still looks at me as if I'm from an alien planet—well, 'cause chicks kinda are, right?—Have you seen us attack chocolate once a month? It's not pretty. But it's not like he'll try to stop me.

As if.

Men don't say to women "That's because you don't have a dick," because not only are we really glad about that for a multitude of reasons that have nothing to do with the goofiness of the term itself, though that definitely has something to do with it, we're just happy our genitals don't pop out like a mouse out of a house.

Let's deconstruct.

My guy will do lots of fun stuff with the kids—bike rides, pool, park. When they get home, they collapse like puppies in an exhausted heap. Does he clean them up, feed them, shower and change them?

Hello, McFly?

When I went to New York City recently for a work trip, I wasn't surprised to come home to a decently clean home, yet children who hadn't been bathed in four days.

Does it just not occur to men to bathe the kids? I give him credit for the feeding and watering of them. He's not a helpless, completely clueless man. But if he had a vagina, would he have remembered to wash them, too?

(Yeah, you don't need to point out to me that if he had a vagina I wouldn't be with him. #Badredhead doesn't swing that way. Not that there's anything wrong with that.)

I look at my side. If I had a dick, would I have taken them for the long bike ride, up and down all those hills? (He's got the boy's bike attached to the back of his). Probably not. He's definitely stronger than I am. Other activities, sure. But it's not a competition.

And that's not my point anyway.

How we care for our kids will always be different, just because as chicks, I'll admit we're always wanting to make sure our kids are clean enough (which is never the case), well-fed, and well-rested. Whereas the guys are moving on to the next activity, the next task on the Honey-Do List, or the next tool to buy for their He-Man Master of the Universe Kit.

No matter how much I fight it, I can't help nurturing these kids. Oh wait, that's what I'm *supposed* to do.

Yeah, right.

Listen, men don't think like us and they never will. Which is fine. Because if they did? We'd just fight over who was gonna mother the kids. Now THAT could get ugly.

THE PENIS. DECONSTRUCTED.

I like to discuss topics that make people uncomfortable. 'Cause it's, ya know, fun.

Take the penis.

That word is just not attractive to chicks. (Especially if you're a lesbian.)

For most females who enjoy hetero sex, I'd say the consensus is to go with *cock*. It's strong and ends with a hard consonant (and it's similar to another word ending in "ck"). And believe me, hard is good for *this* conversation.

Penis is so clinical. It's not sexy, hot, or engaging in any way. And that snaky "s" at the end doesn't do it any favors.

I don't know. "Would you like to have sex with my penis?" just doesn't do it for a girl, somehow. It's sort of wimpy, ya know? Like asking to pay for your cheeseburger on Tuesday while you eat it today. That's a no-fly zone.

Dick has too many negative connotations. I always feel sorry for any Richards I meet. And poor Andy Dick. He should marry a nice girl (or boy), and change his name.

No matter what you believe about how we got here, men's business is not the prettiest sight to look at. Put that shit away, bros. If you must whip it out, have the courtesy to manscape that mess.

And the whole popping up at inopportune times thing. What's up with that? We girls cannot relate. It's not like boobs do that. I mean sure, our nips get hard, but so what? You guys dig that. (We can tell by how your penis pops up.)

Sure, chicks can be ruled by our hormones. I own my bitchiness at that time of the month. I have a right to it at this point, baby. We're emotional creatures and yeah, we're always cold. (Or hot. Or cold.) But that doesn't hold a candle to watching someone walk by and having a body part spring up to march like a soldier off to war.

We can't imagine what it's like to be you and have something with a mind of its own making your decisions. Of course, not that all men are like that. That would be stereotyping and I don't mean to imply that men don't think with their brains.

I know lots of men who never think about sex.

I'm sorry. Can't stop laughing.

Not that it's your fault or that we blame you. We just like to laugh at you about something you can't control (like your ear hair).

We appreciate that you're attracted to us after all these years, childbirth and all; even if you're as excited by those <u>Victoria's Secret models</u> as you are by the grocery store cashier. We don't take it personally.

We love that you're still into us. Know your left from your other left. And we're just happy you still know your penis from our vagina.

THE VAGINA. DECONSTRUCTED.

Don't you just love to discuss things that make other people squirm? Maybe it's a redhead thing.

Like how seventy-five to eighty percent of women have orgasms via <u>clitoral stimulation</u>. This seems to surprise a lot of people. Especially men, some who have disagreed with me vehemently. 'Cause, ya know, doctors and scientists and, I don't know, WOMEN, must all be wrong about how our own bodies work.

Women love that.

Let's discuss the word *vagina*. For such a hot, amazing, mystical, bitchin' place, the word itself, um, blows.

Vagina literally means "split sheath." Those Latins took everything so seriously.

Now there's a sexy party for ya.

There is clearly nothing seductive about the word vagina. Though sometimes it does come in handy in a humorous, Chickspeak vs. Mancode-type situation, as in:

Husband: I don't understand why chicks are always talking about sex.

Me: That's 'cause you don't have a vagina.

So for effect, the word can be used quite adequately in a well-placed barb.

But when it comes to enticing your partner? "Honey, do you want to get inside my hot vagina?" just doesn't do it for either of us. It feels a little #BigBangTheory Amy Farrah-Fowler like, to be honest. (*Sheldon, I'll be over in twenty minutes for our weekly coitus date in my vagina. Eat your cereal. I recommend the box at the high-fiber end of the spectrum for maximum performance.*)

Then again, I've never known a guy to say no to *anything* having to do with sex.

Still.

The problem is, there aren't a lot of words for the female genitalia that are acceptable to most chicks. My one girlfriend is so offended by the word *pussy* that she throws up in her mouth a little whenever her husband (or really anyone) calls it that. *Cunt* isn't much better—most women are so incredibly offended by that word, I'll probably get hate mail just for daring to write it down.

Here's my feeling. Call it whatever you want. Some people name theirs (really, don't share). Some give out wayyyy too much info about all the names they call it, all its many talents, or how in college it learned to tie a cherry stem into a knot.

TMI.

The point is this. A woman's hoo-ha is a powerful, magical place (unless, ya know, you're a gay man. But even he came from somewhere.), capable of giving and receiving pleasure; *and* childbirth. It's a little mind-blowing.

To be honest, I can understand why people have pet names for it. It responds well to attention, especially if you groom it, stroke it, and feed it.

Give the kitty what it wants and she will purr for you.

Though I do draw the line at the taking it for a walk part.

MEN NEED ROUTINE

Men need routine.

Everyone knows kids need routine. That goes without saying. Plenty of studies on that.

No, I'm talking about the big guys.

If my guy can't be asleep by 9:30 p.m. each night, he's Mr. Crankypants the next day. Granted, he's up at 4:30 a.m. to deal with East Coast clients. But it kind of puts a dent in our social calendar. On the weekends. When he doesn't have to be up early.

It even makes TV viewing difficult if the kids and I stay up late. Funny how he'll listen to his shows so loud my mom up in Northern California can hear them but when we want to watch a show, I'll get a text (yes, a text), "TURN IT DOWN," when it's already so low we're reading lips.

Sigh.

Men need routine.

I drink my coffee at home. I have Joey the Coffeemaker who greets me every morning with "How you doin'?" What girl doesn't want an Italian Stallion (okay, he's invisible. What's your point?) as she shuffles up in scary hair, morning tee and sweats? My guy, however, is constantly bugging me to get dressed (gasp!) and join him at Starbucks. Why on earth would I want to do that?

Doesn't he know I'm a writer?

Okay, so maybe I need a routine, too. But we're talking about him. What is it about his insistence that we go to Starbucks?

"I love the whole atmosphere—lots of noisy people, the music, the activity, the grinder, the interaction. It's how I start my day, every day. Without it, I just can't get going. Why can't you understand this?" He asks in frustration.

I know he loves me and wants us to spend kid-free time together. I get that. And I love him for it.

I also recoil in horror. Doesn't he know I'm a writer?

"Babe, I get your need for socialism. Okay, wait. Let me rephrase that," I say, looking for a smile. Nothing. Tough crowd.

"You know I'm a social chick. I have my social times. But writing is not one of them. If I wanted to be social, I would have picked a different profession, like math or something. Er, maybe not. And while I love you to death, you don't leave me alone when we go to Starbucks. I can't get anything done," I explain.

He nods. He knows I'm right. (Of course I am. Pft.)

There's something he doesn't realize about his Starbucks routine that's bright as day to me. He'll get his crap done if I'm not there. He may want me there, but he's got deadlines just as I do. And being a one-man show, it's even more critical that he do his own thing.

Men need routine.

Carving out time together with two careers and two kids is tricky, but we do it. Routines keep this democracy from crumbling.

Sometimes we deviate of course. Illnesses, vacations, when the kids have days off school—which just screws everything up.

And sometimes I go with him. Sure, I love to hang out with him. And sometimes I really, really want a piece of pumpkin bread.

Look for part three of **The Chronicles of Snark** next year with *Chickspeak: Uncovered.*

RACHEL THOMPSON

Website:

http://RachelintheOC.com

Facebook:

https://www.facebook.com/RachelThompsonauthor

Twitter:

http://twitter.com/rachelintheoc

LinkedIn:

http://www.linkedin.com/pub/rachel-thompson/24/784/b95

Pinterest:

http://pinterest.com/rachelintheoc/

MORE GREAT READS FROM BOOKTROPE

Scars from a Memoir by **Marni Mann** (Contemporary Fiction) Sometimes our choices leave scars. For heroin addict Nicole, staying sober will be the fight of her life. But having lost so much, can she afford to lose anything else?

Spots Blind by **Linda Lavid** (Fiction - Short Stories) Stories about being blindsided—sometimes by family, friends, and lovers; sometimes by our own refusal to see the truth.

Summer of Government Cheese by **Paula Marie Coomer** (Fiction - Short Stories) A collection of darkly introspective short stories. As they say, one way to dispel darkness is to expose it to light.

The Dead Boy's Legacy by **Cassius Shuman** (Fiction) 9-year-old Tommy McCarthy is abducted while riding his bike home from a little league game. This psychological family drama explores his family's grief while also looking at the background and motivations of his abductor.

I Kidnap Girls: Stealing from Traffickers, Restoring their Victims by **Pamela Ravan-Pyne and Iana Matei** (Fictionalized Biography) How a phone call to one woman resulted in the rescue of over 400 victims of forced prostitution.

Behind the Shades: Hope Beyond Darkness by **Sheila Raye Charles and Glenn Swanson** (Personal Memoir) Being the daughter of a famous musician is not always what it seems. A story of hope beyond the darkness.

Suitcase Filled with Nails: Lessons Learned from Teaching Art in Kuwait by **Yvonne Wakefield** (Personal Memoir) Leaving behind a secure life in the Pacific Northwest, Yvonne Wakefield finds both joy and struggle in teaching art to young women in Kuwait. A colorful, true, and riveting tale of living and coping in the Middle East.

Discover more books and learn about our
new approach to publishing at **booktrope.com**.

CPSIA information can be obtained
at www.ICGtesting.com
Printed in the USA
FFOW04n1850190614
5976FF

9 781620 151600